My Relaxing Coloring Book

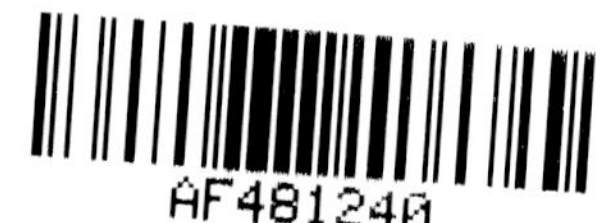

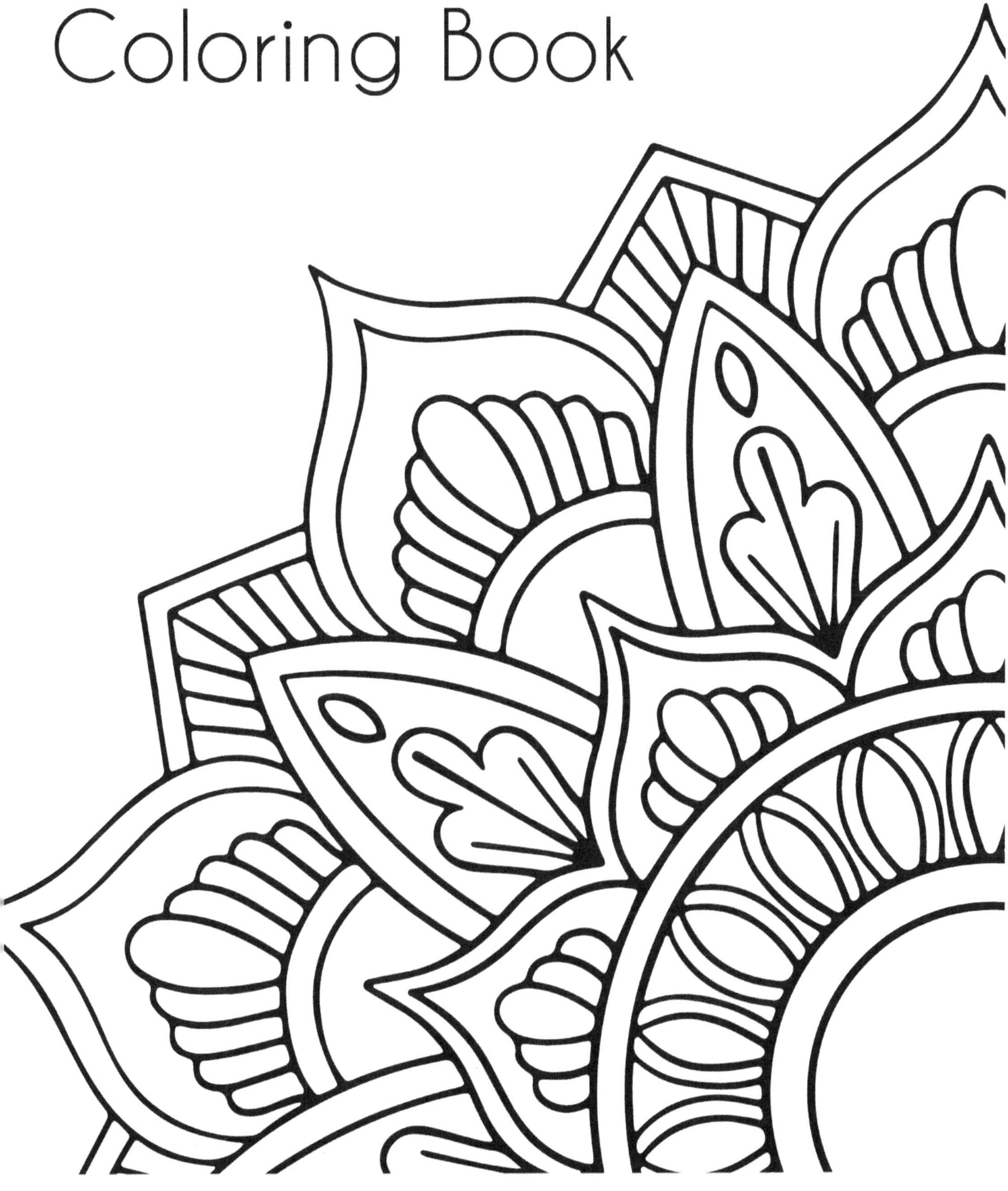

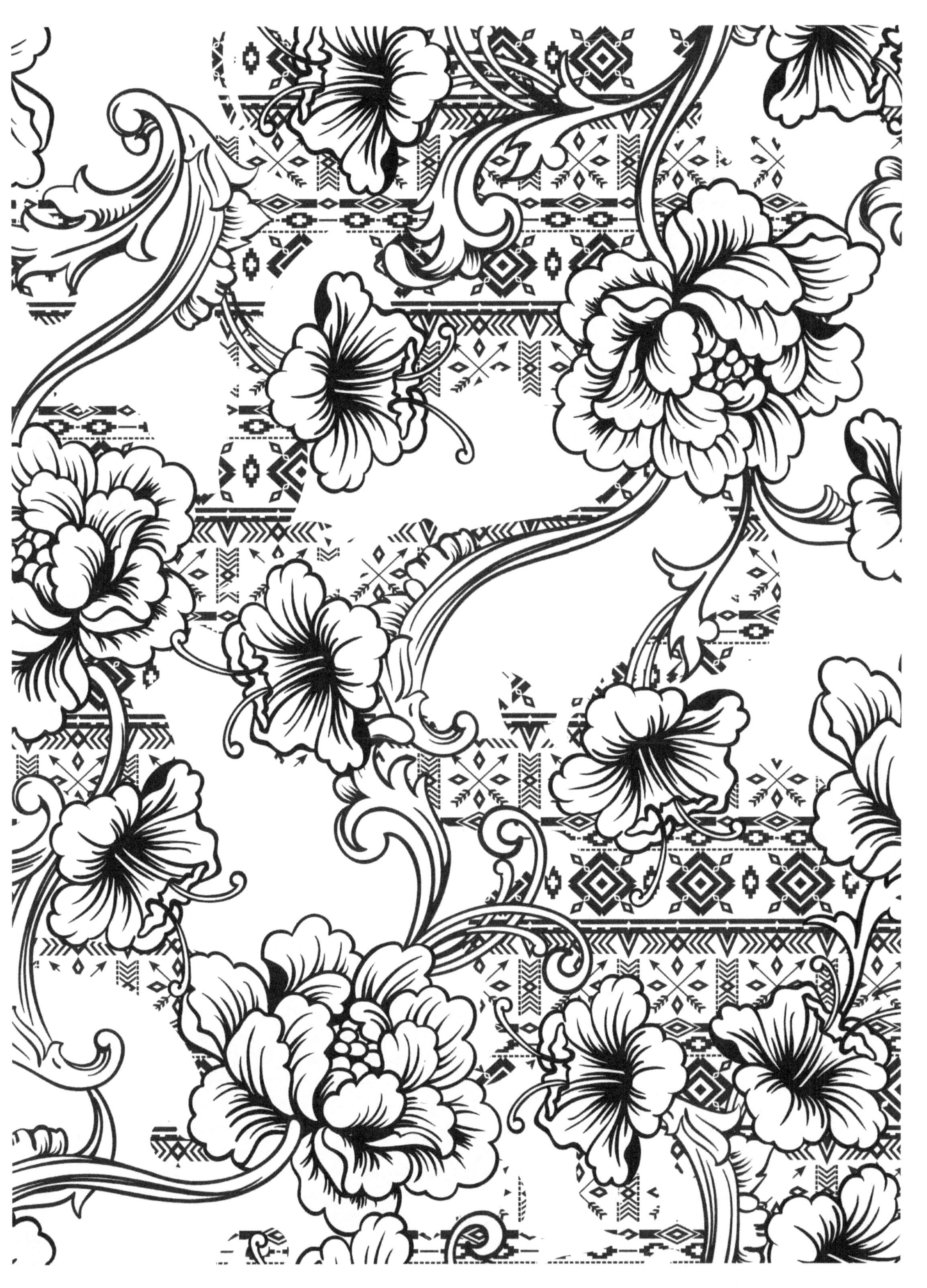

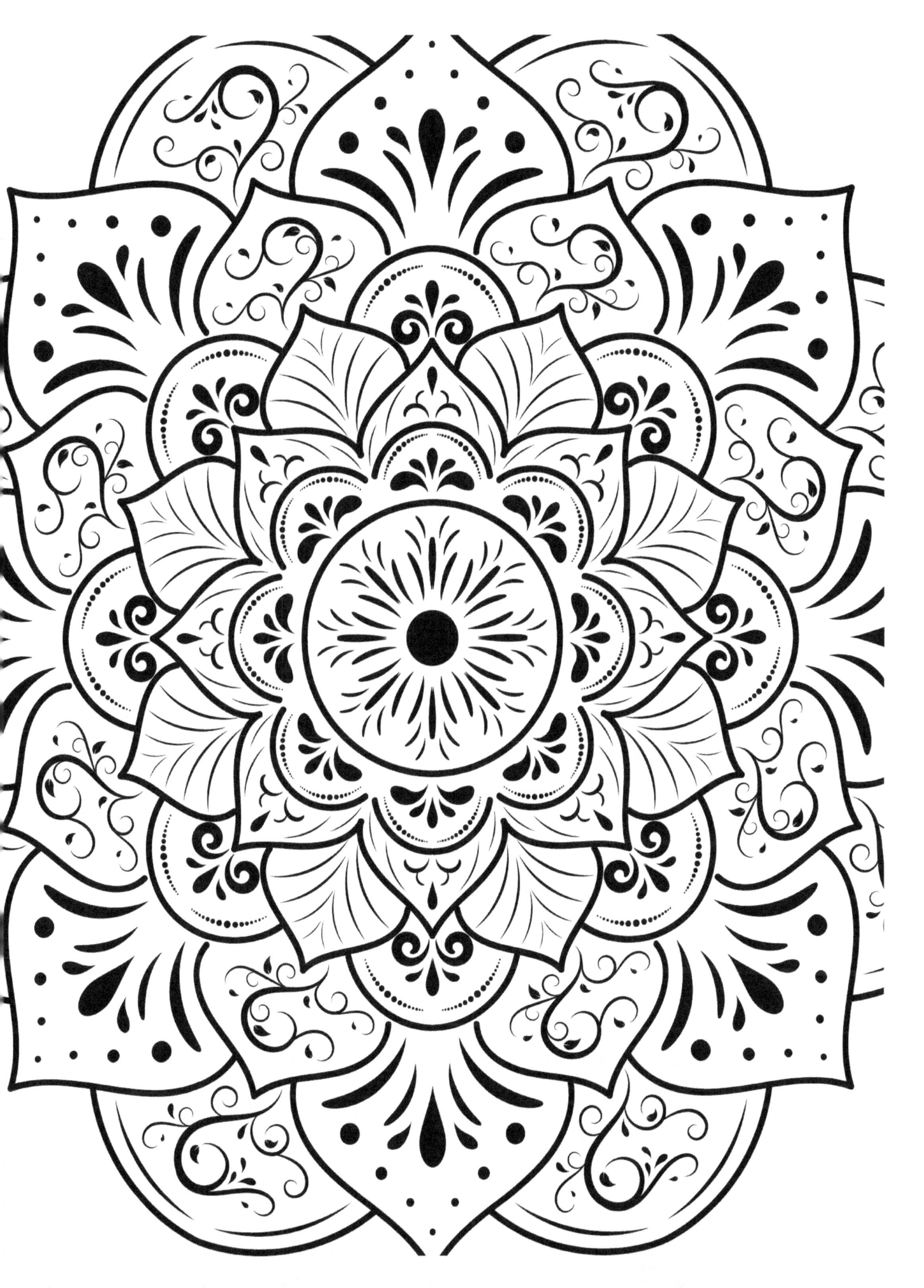

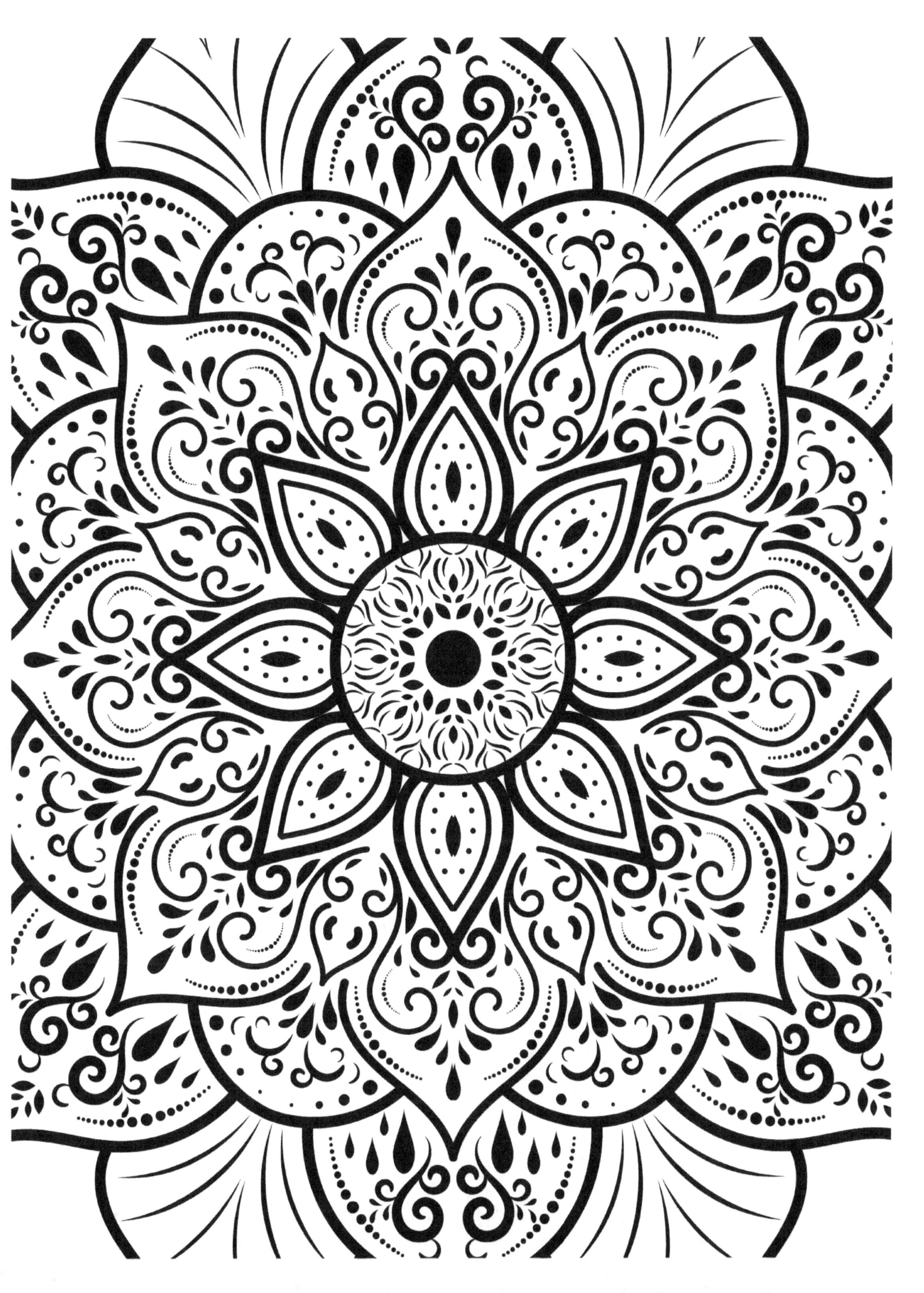

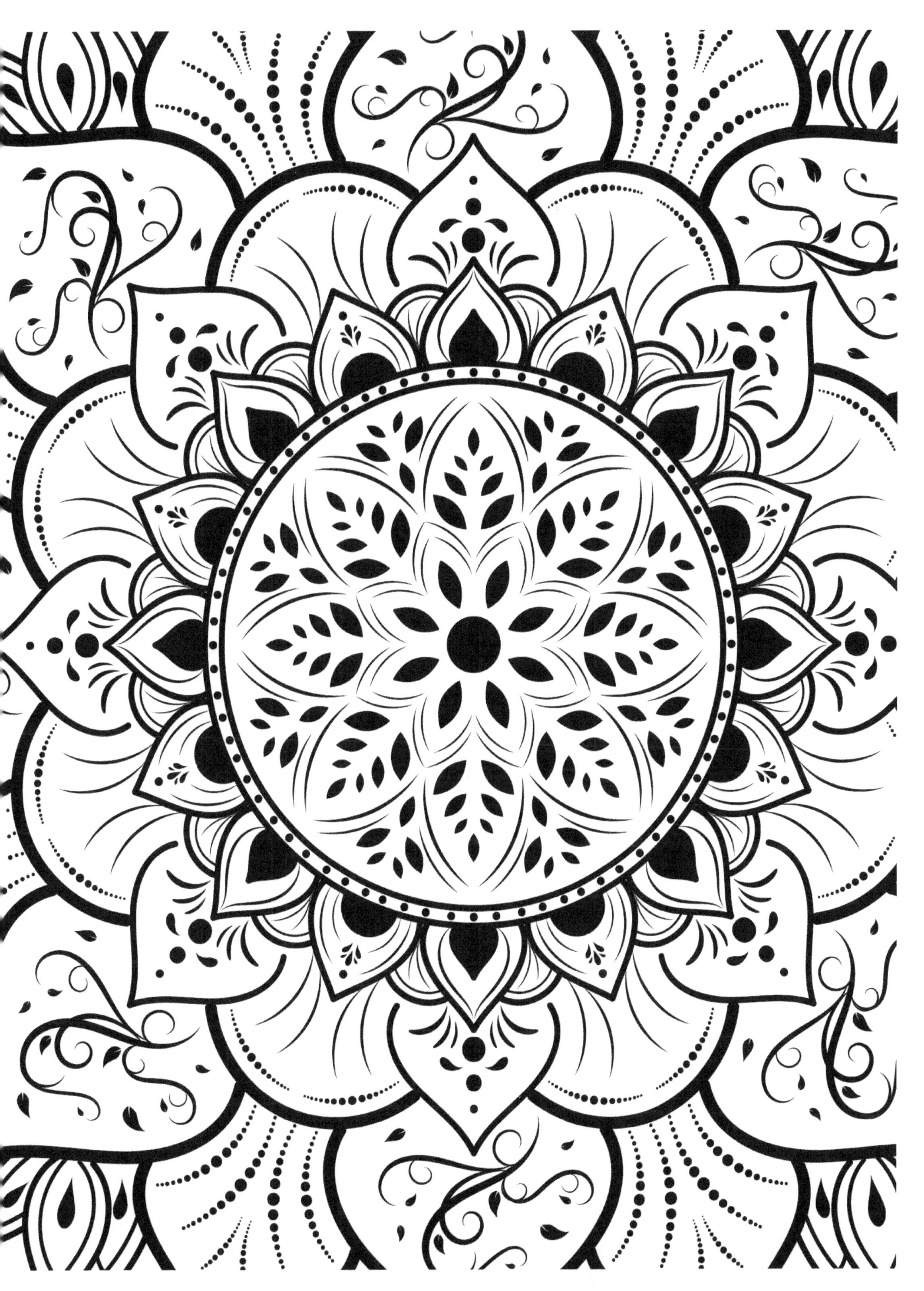

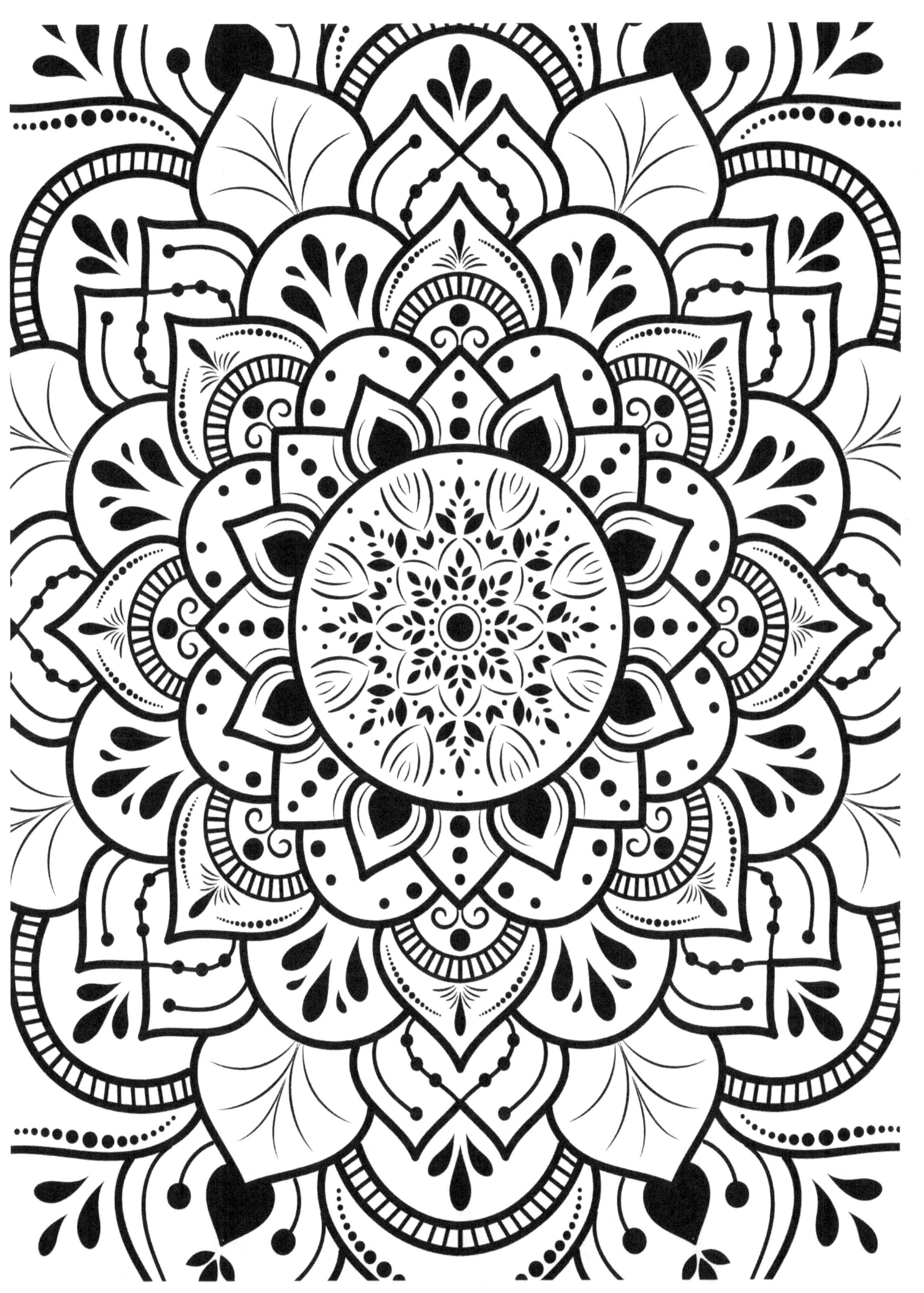

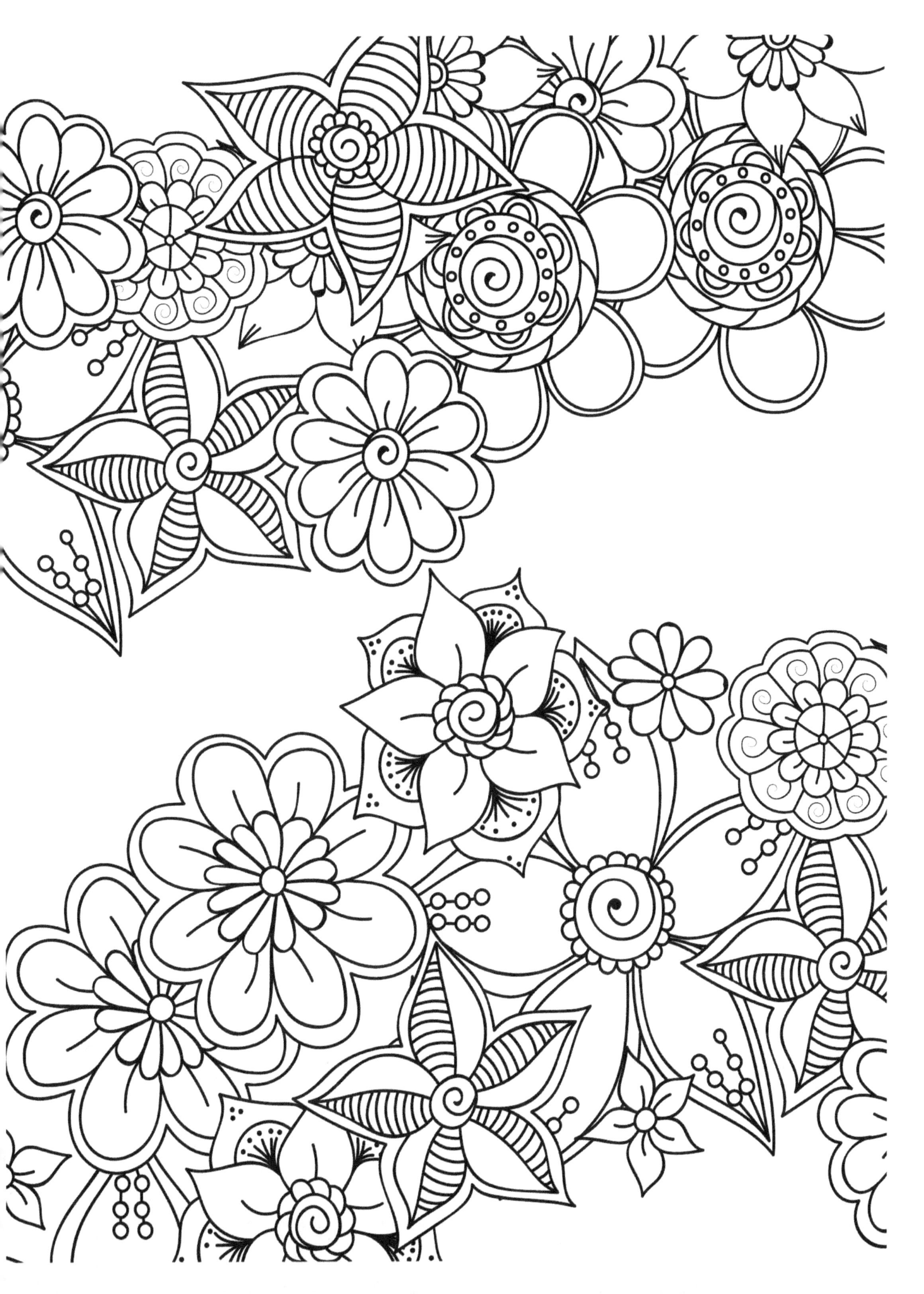

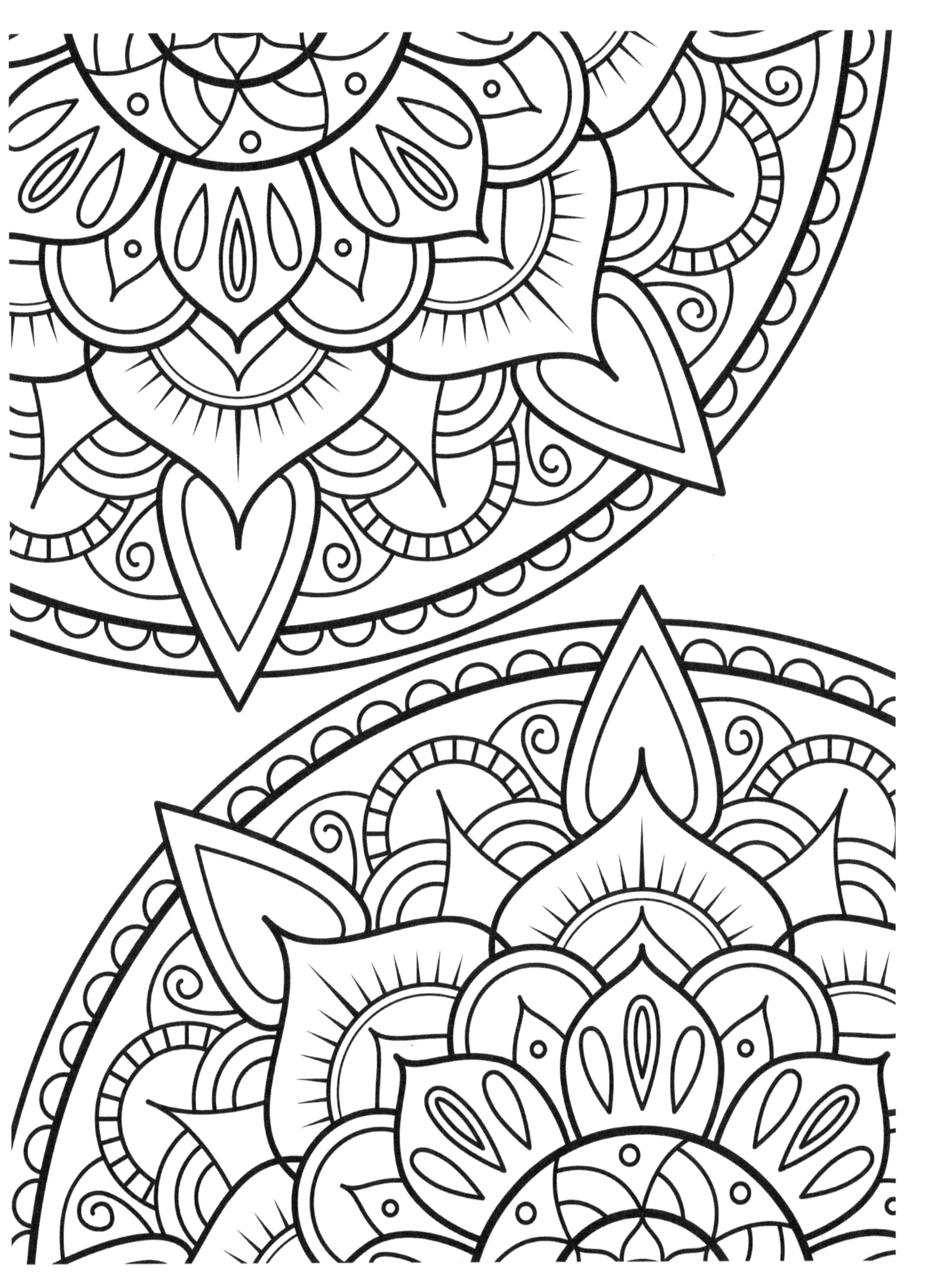

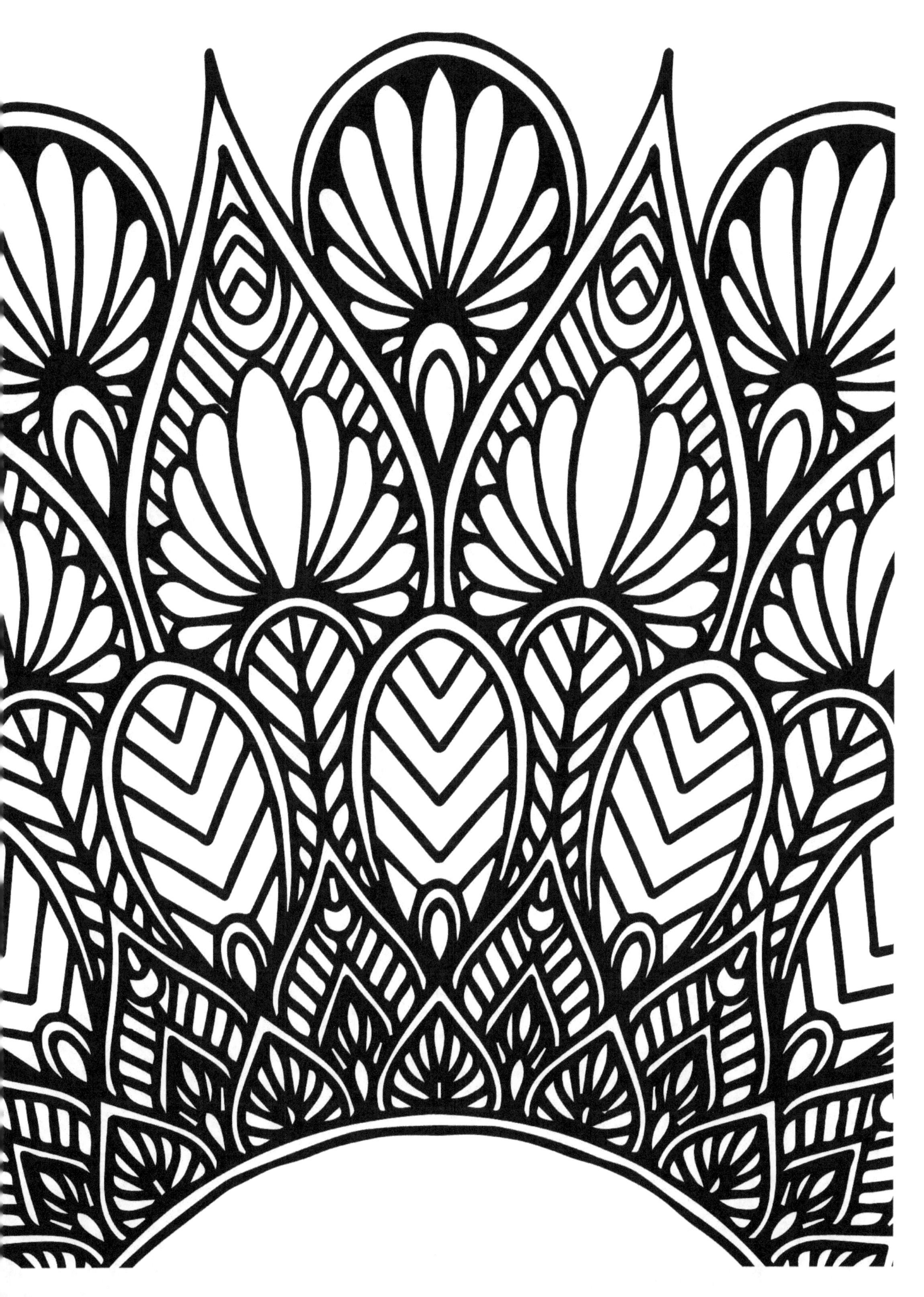

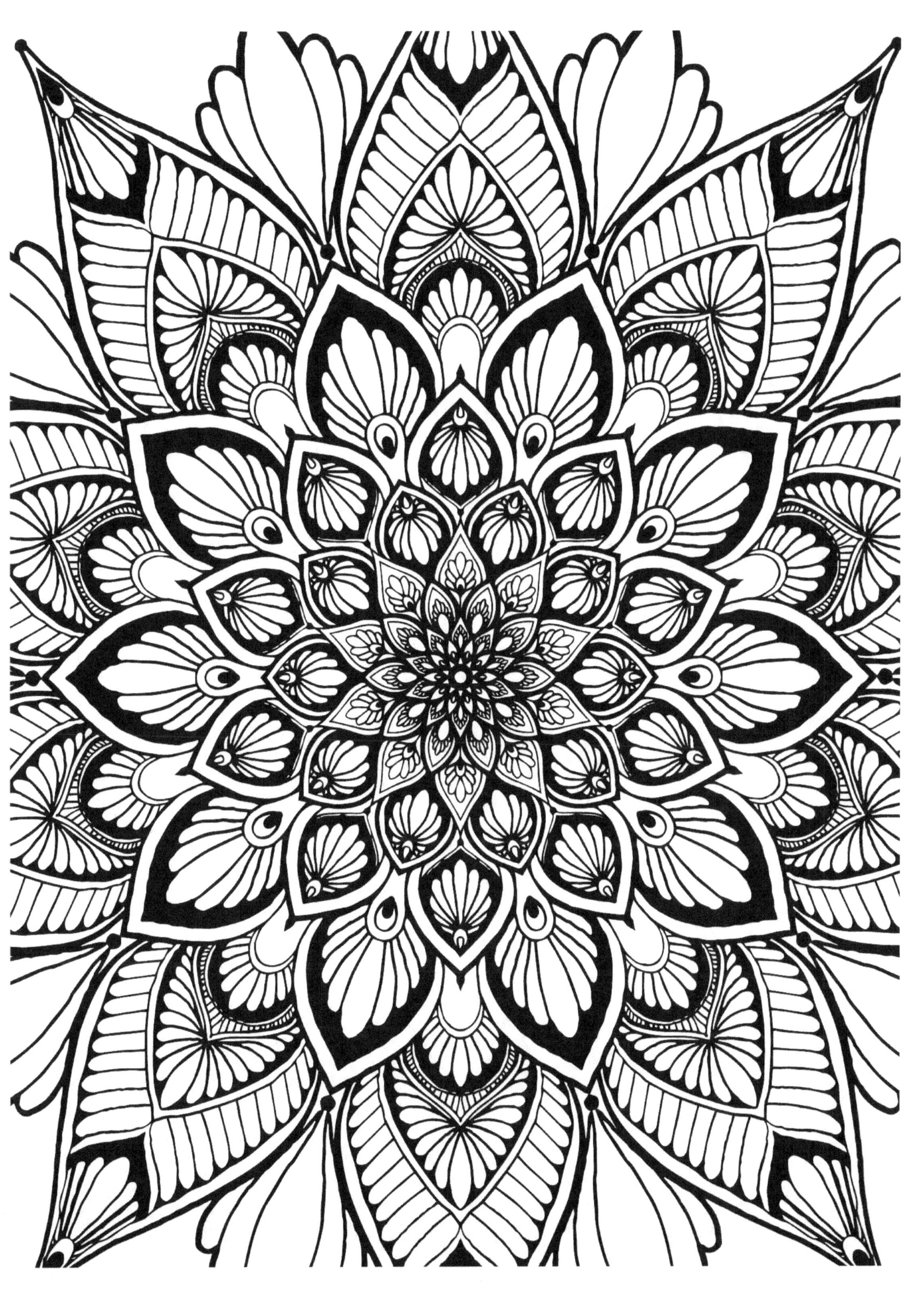

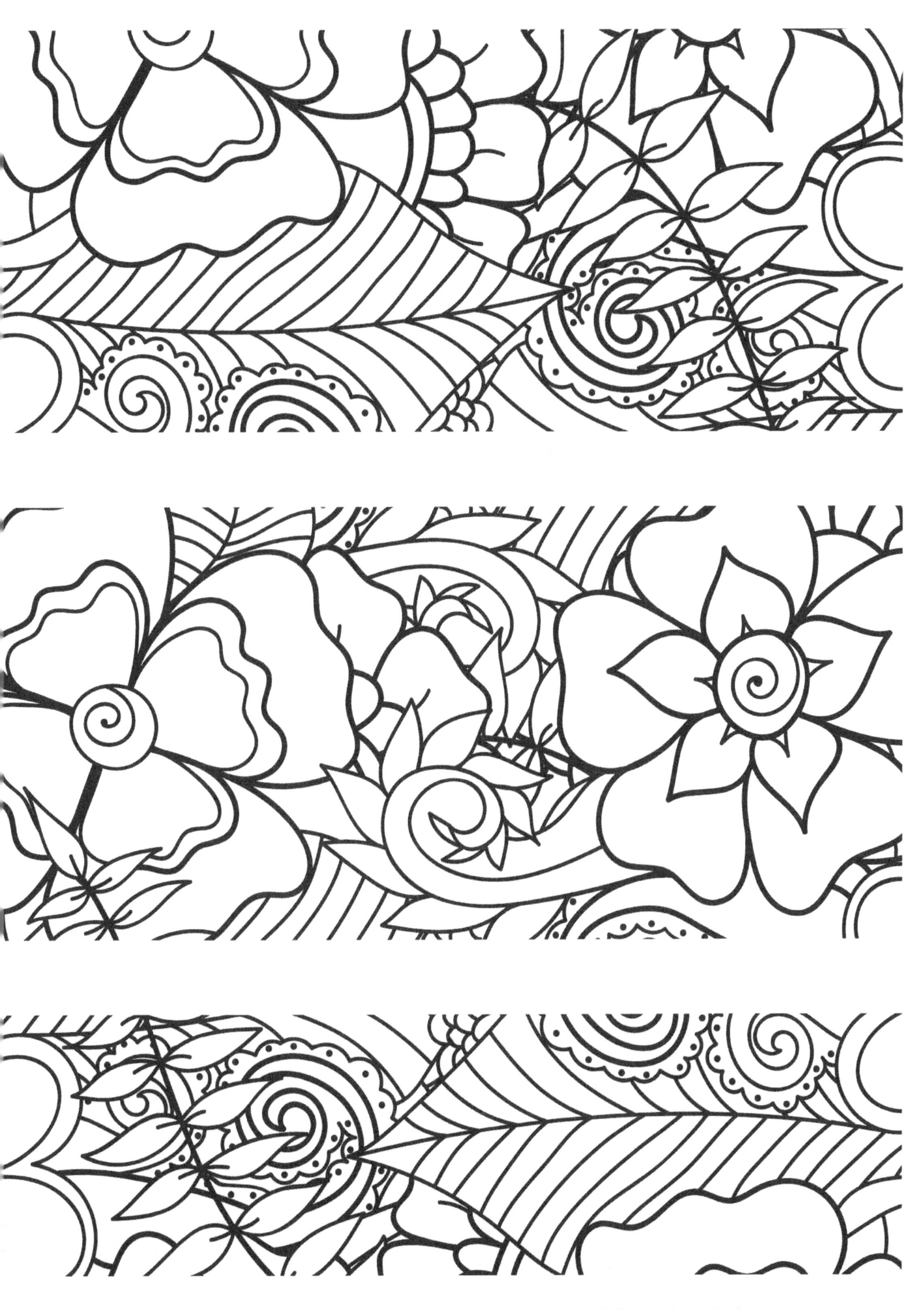

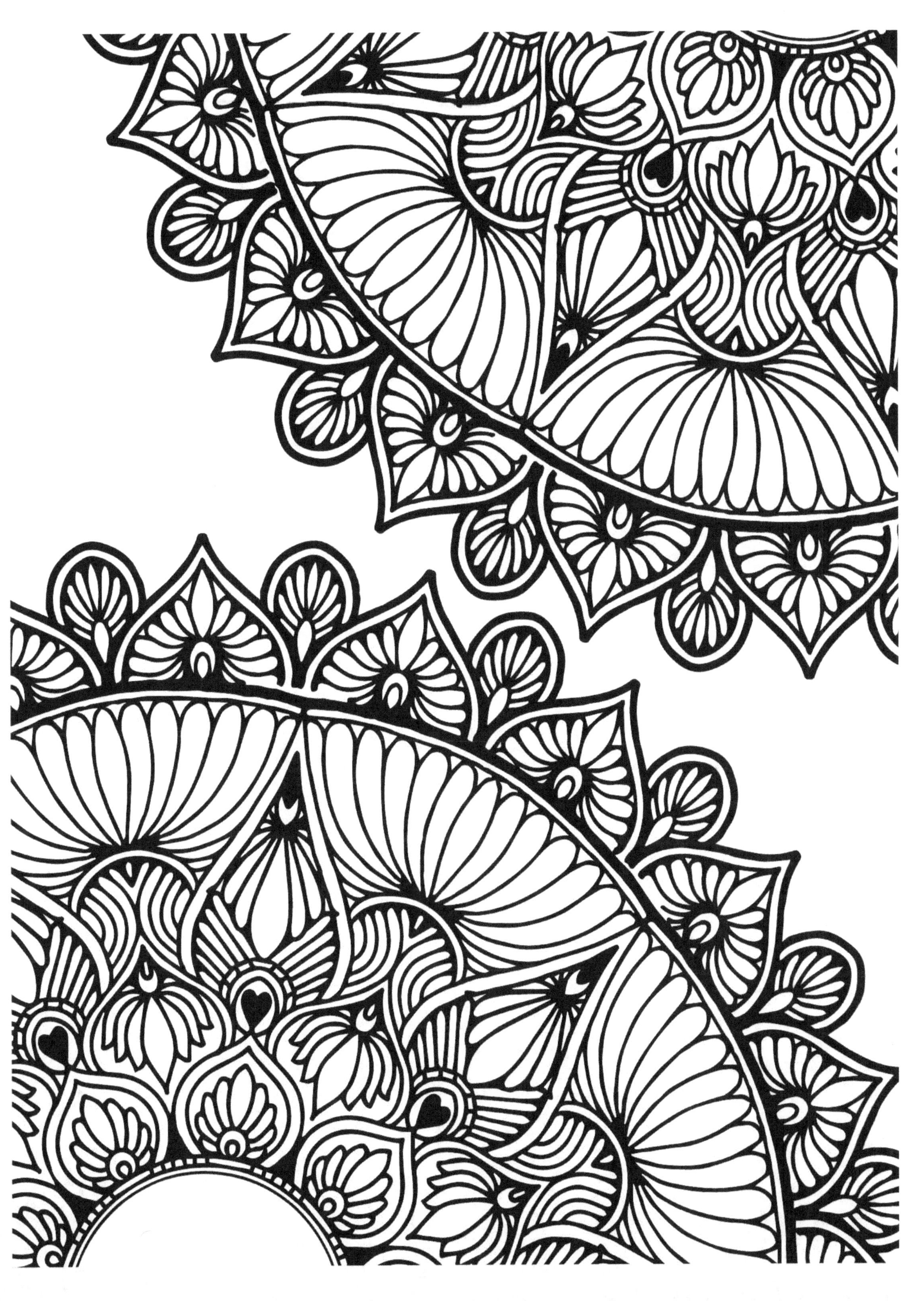

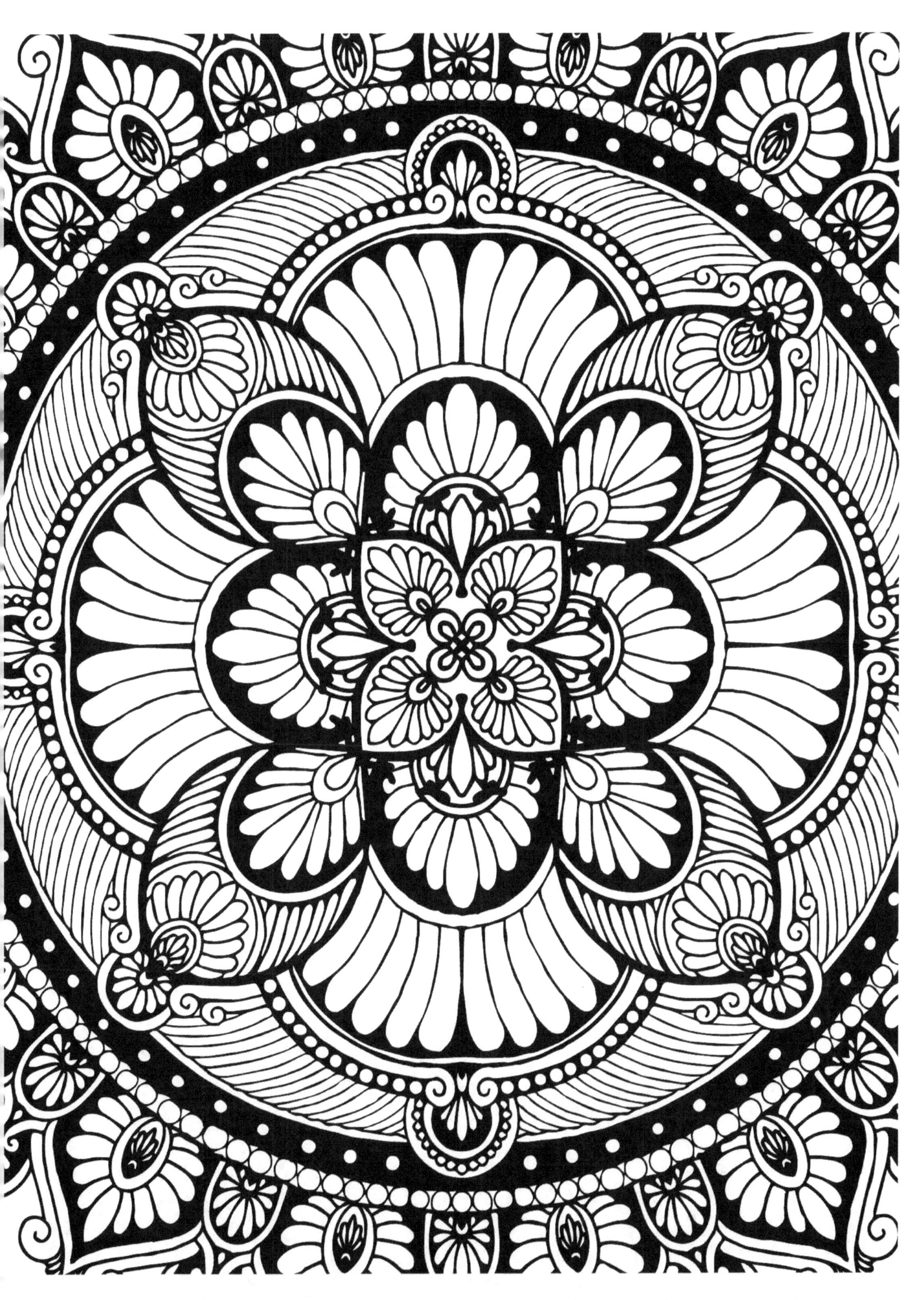

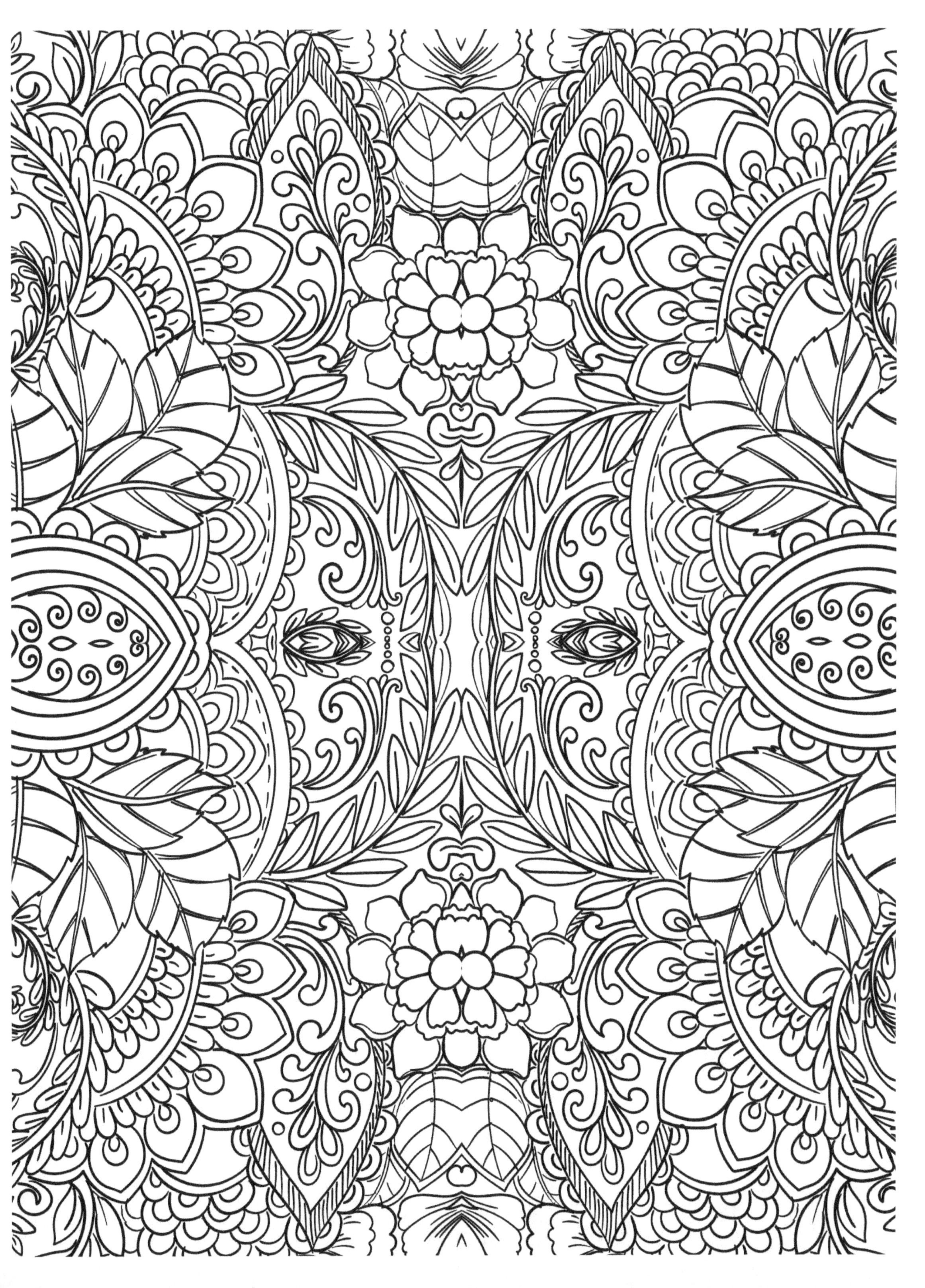

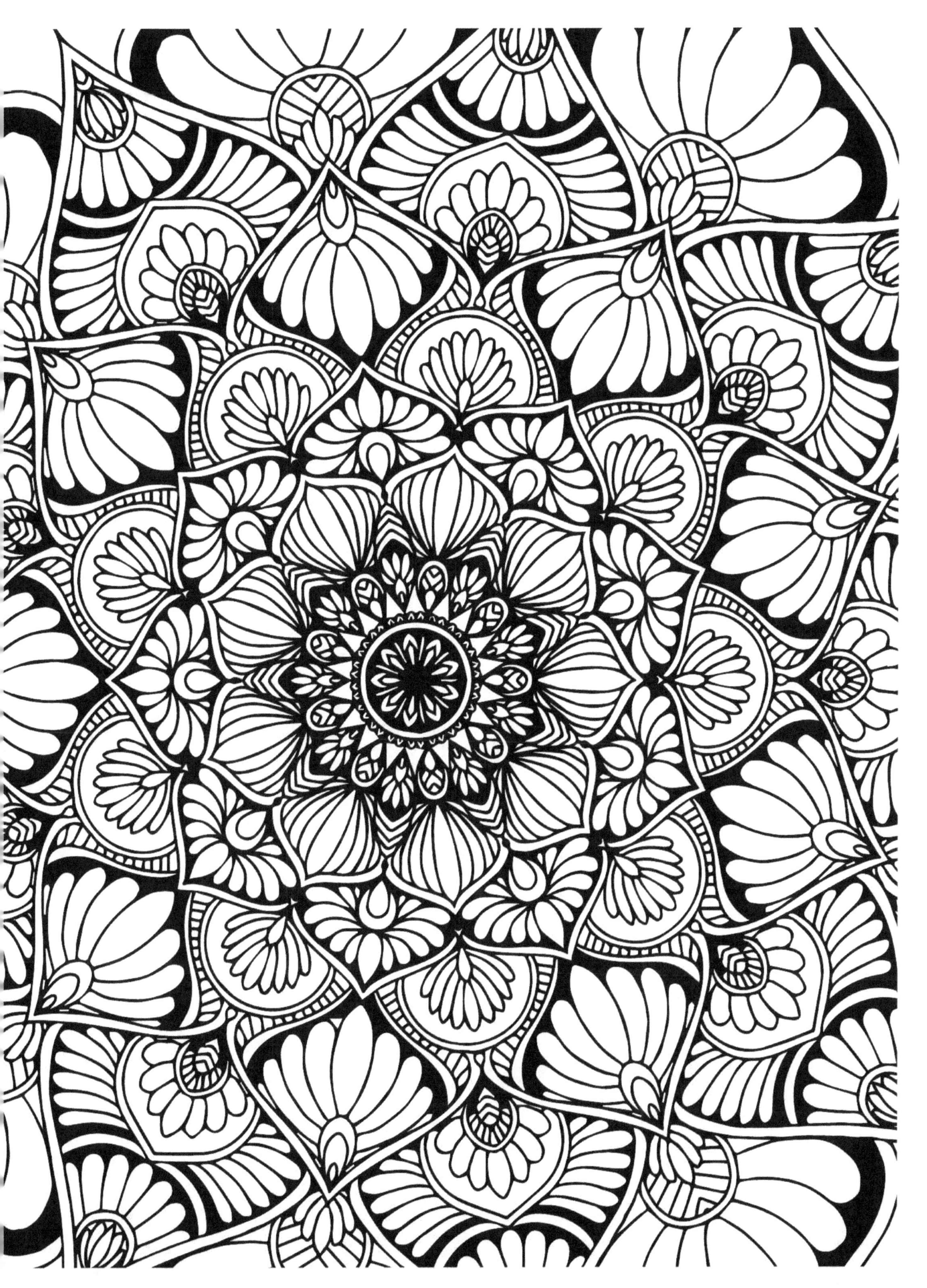

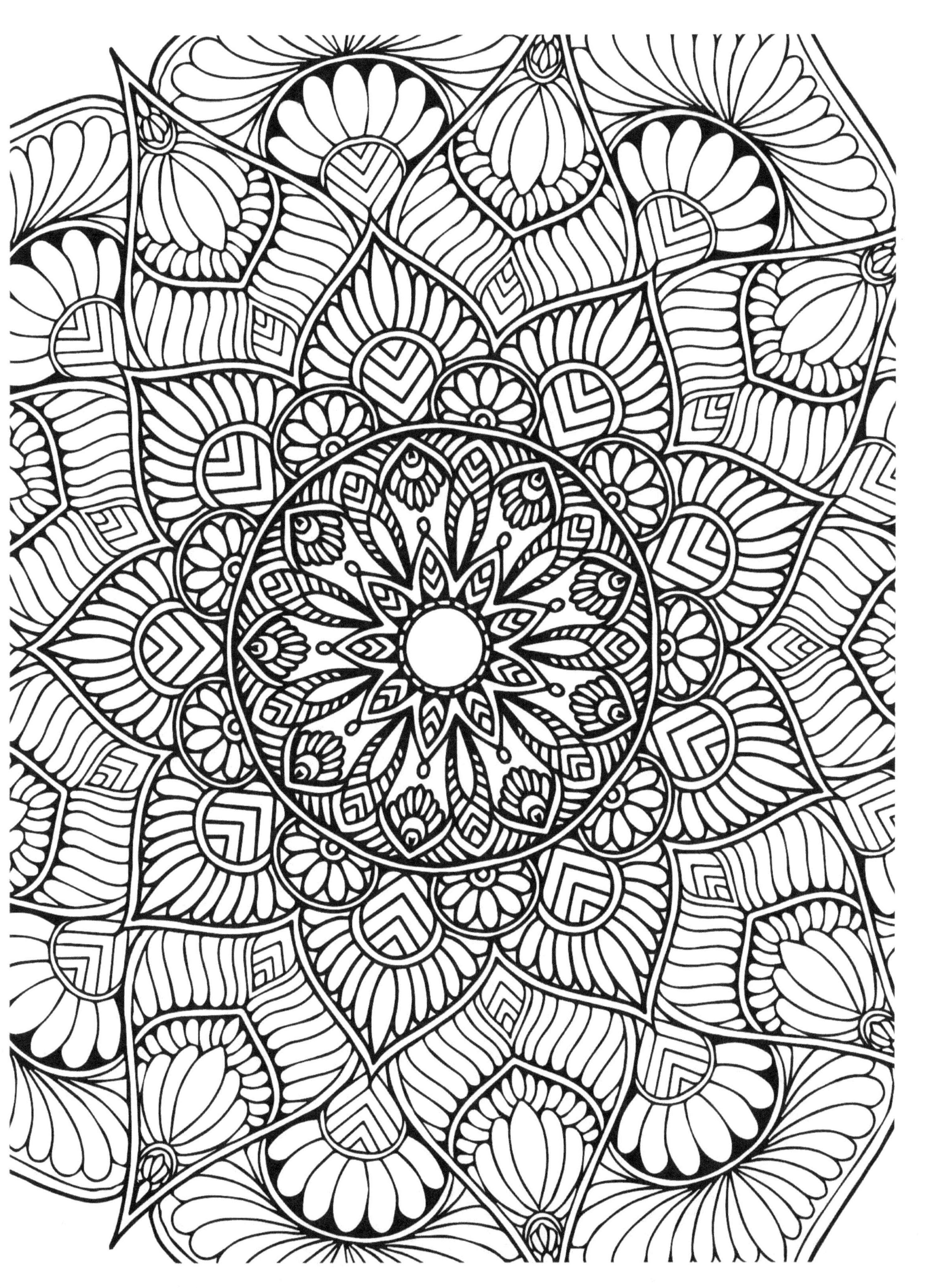

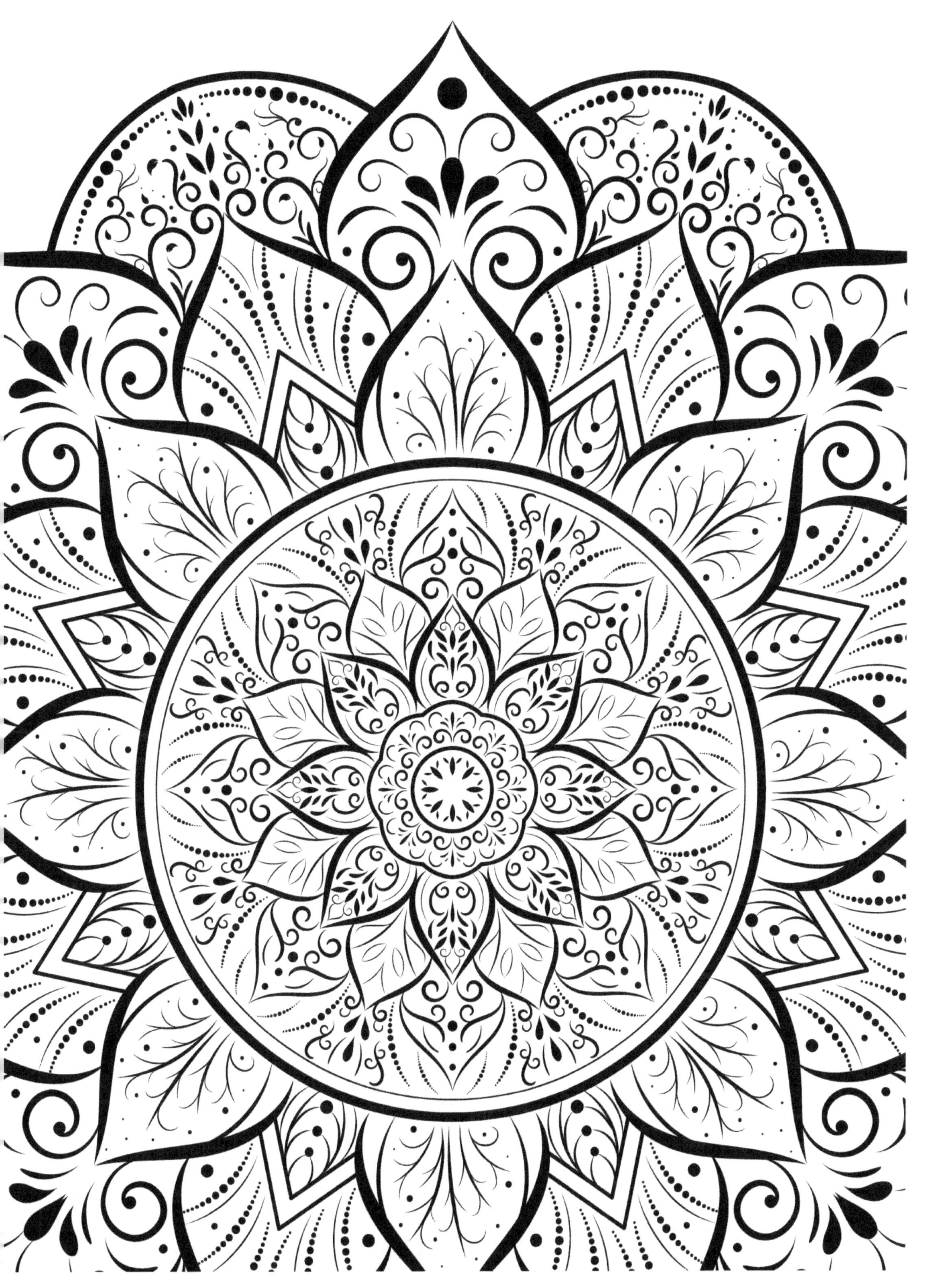

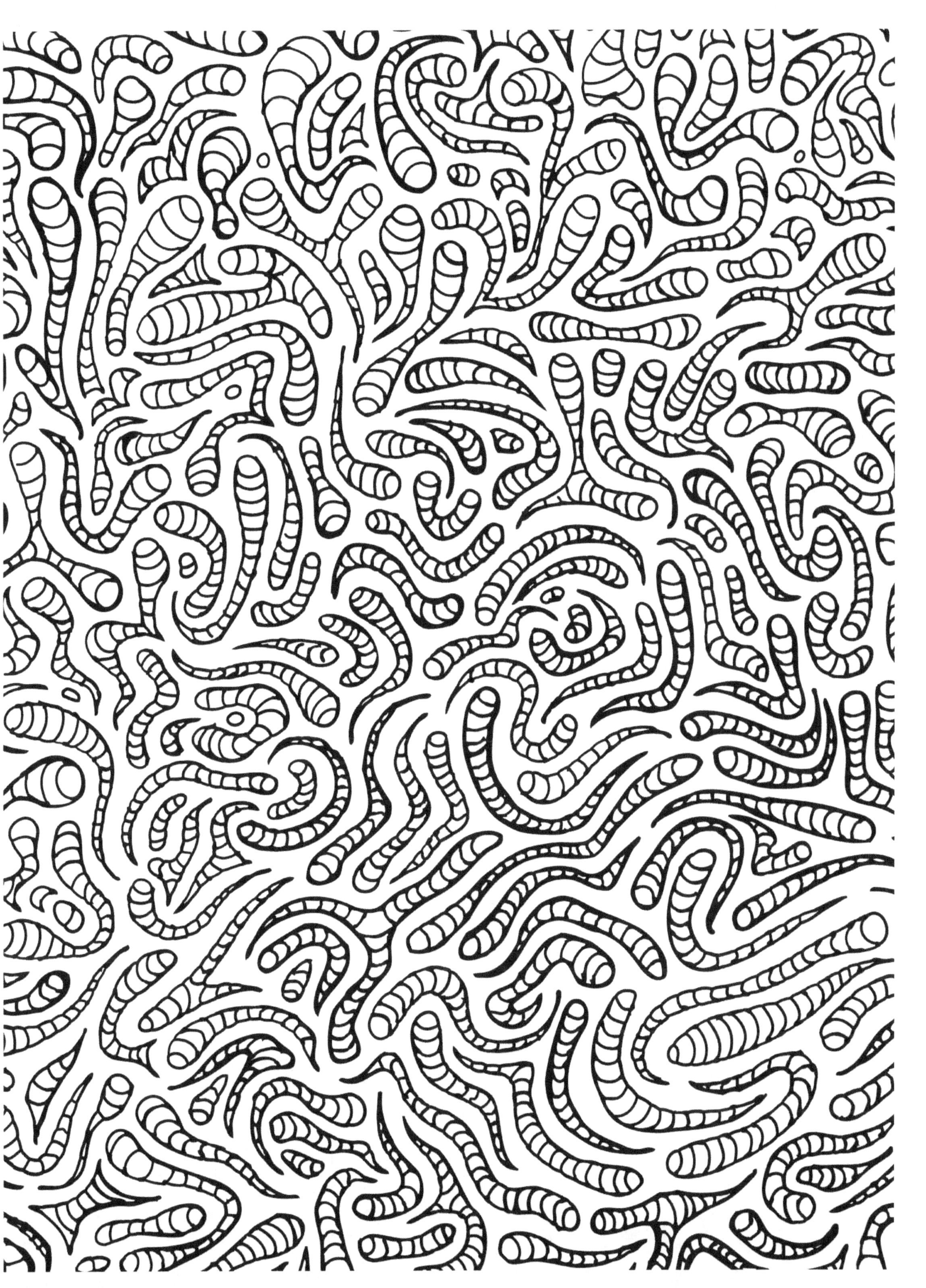

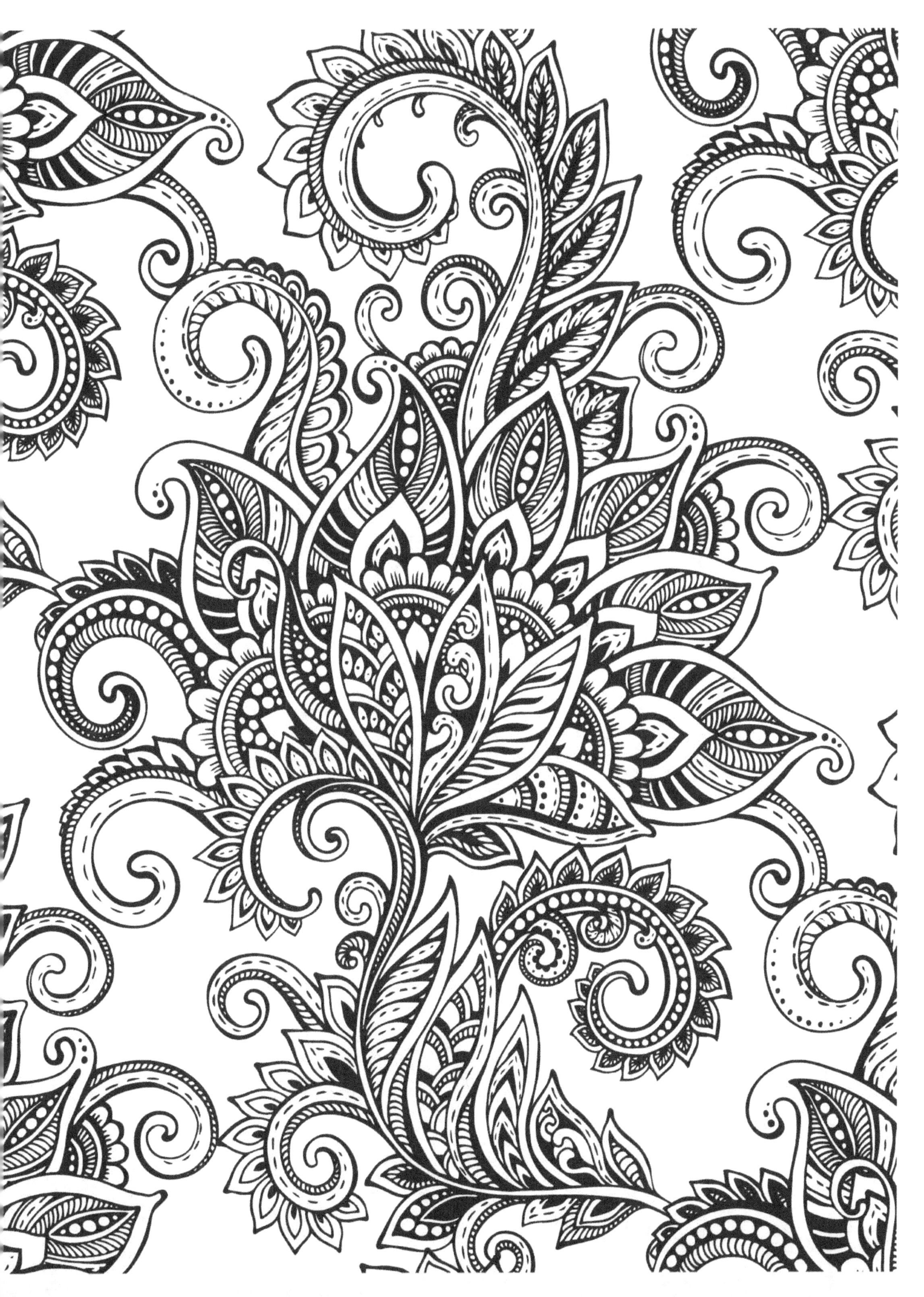

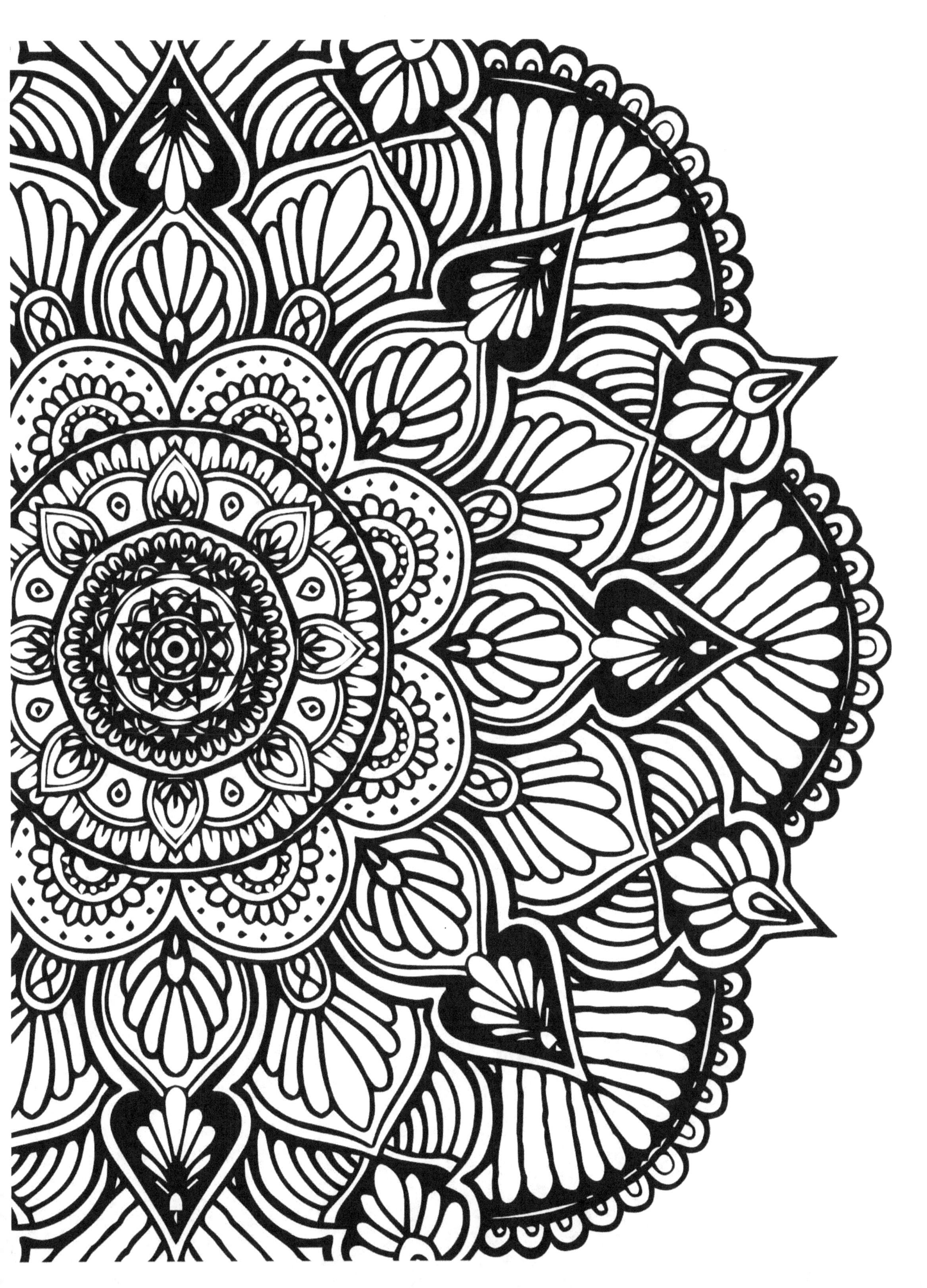

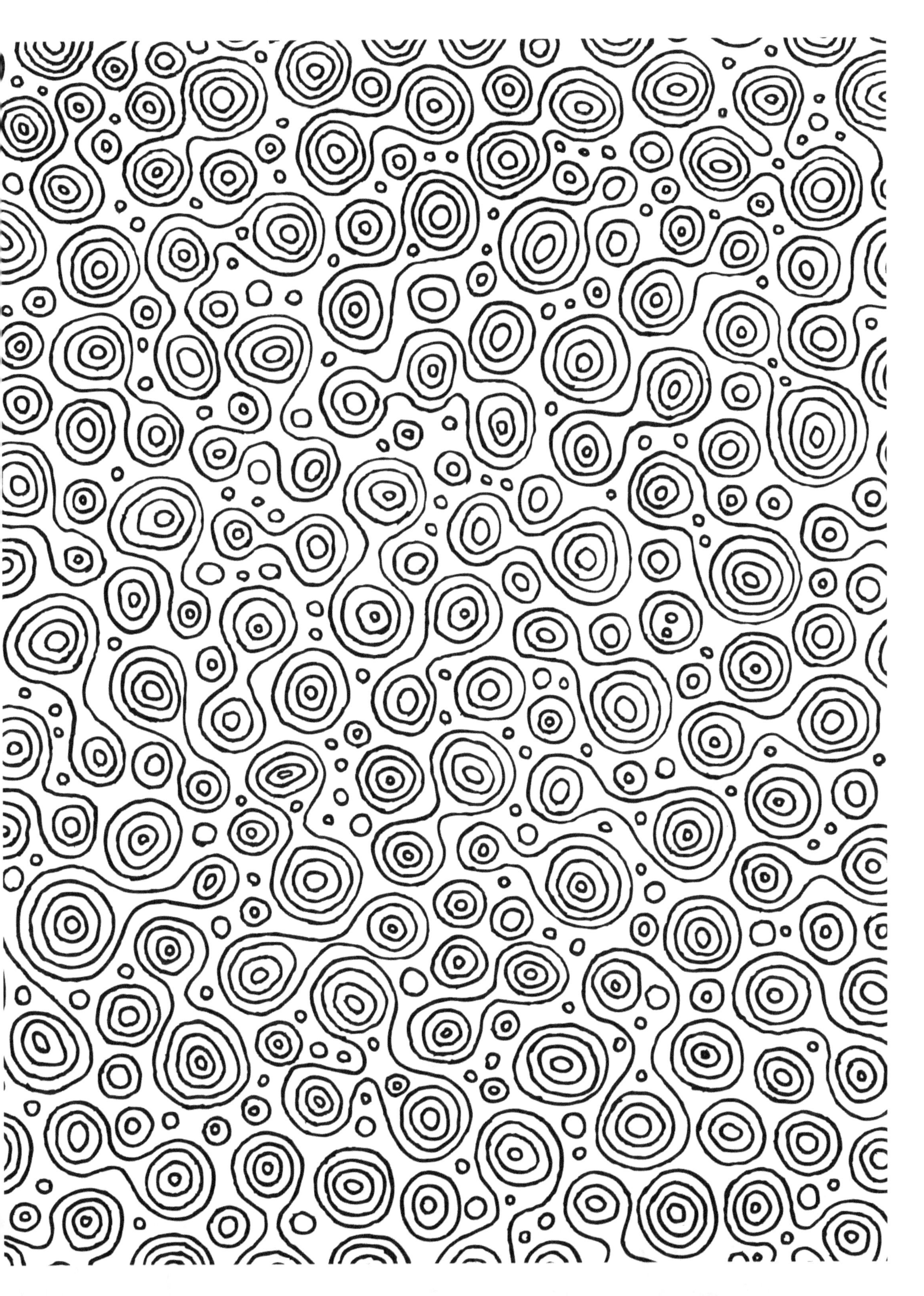

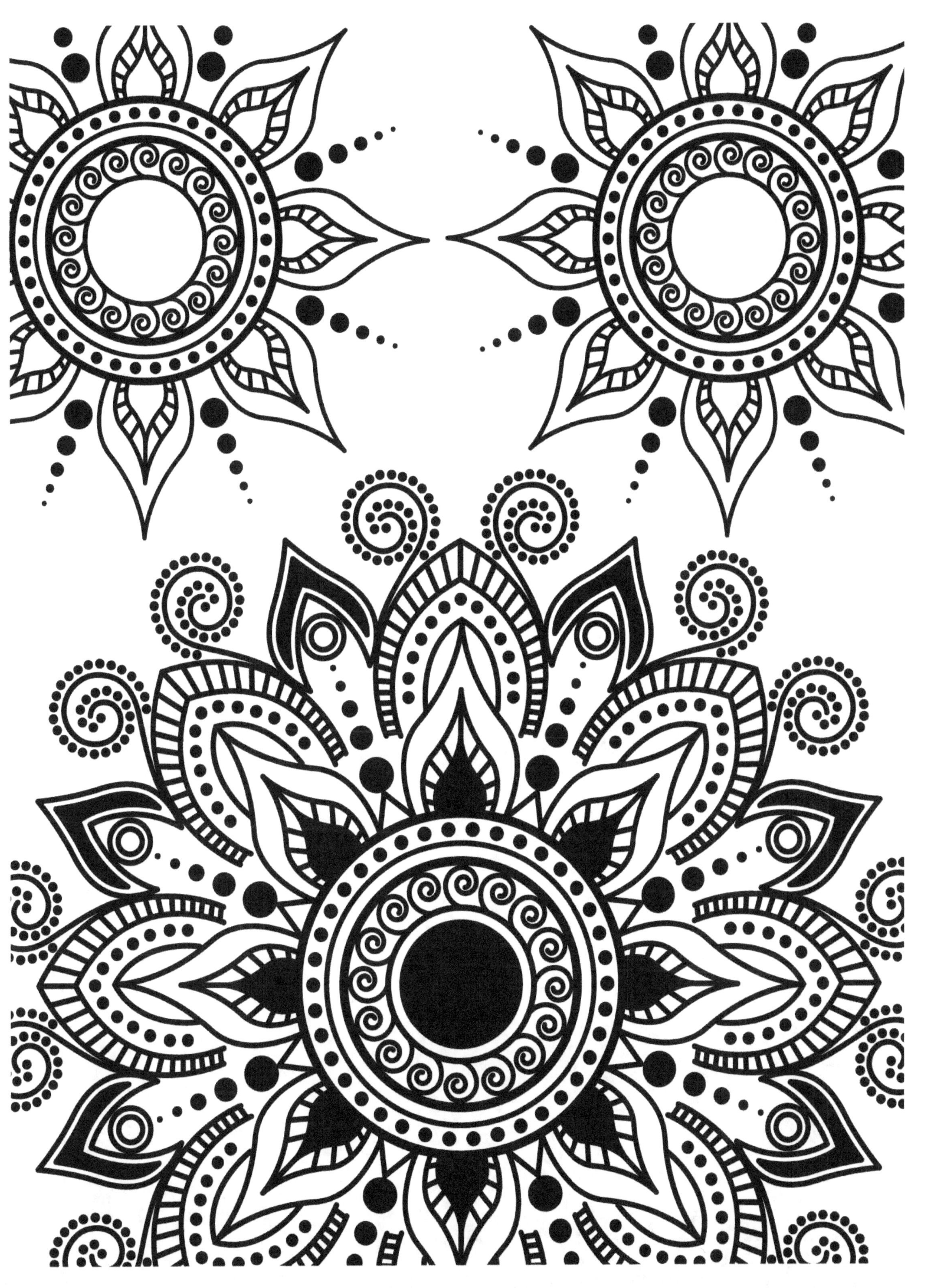

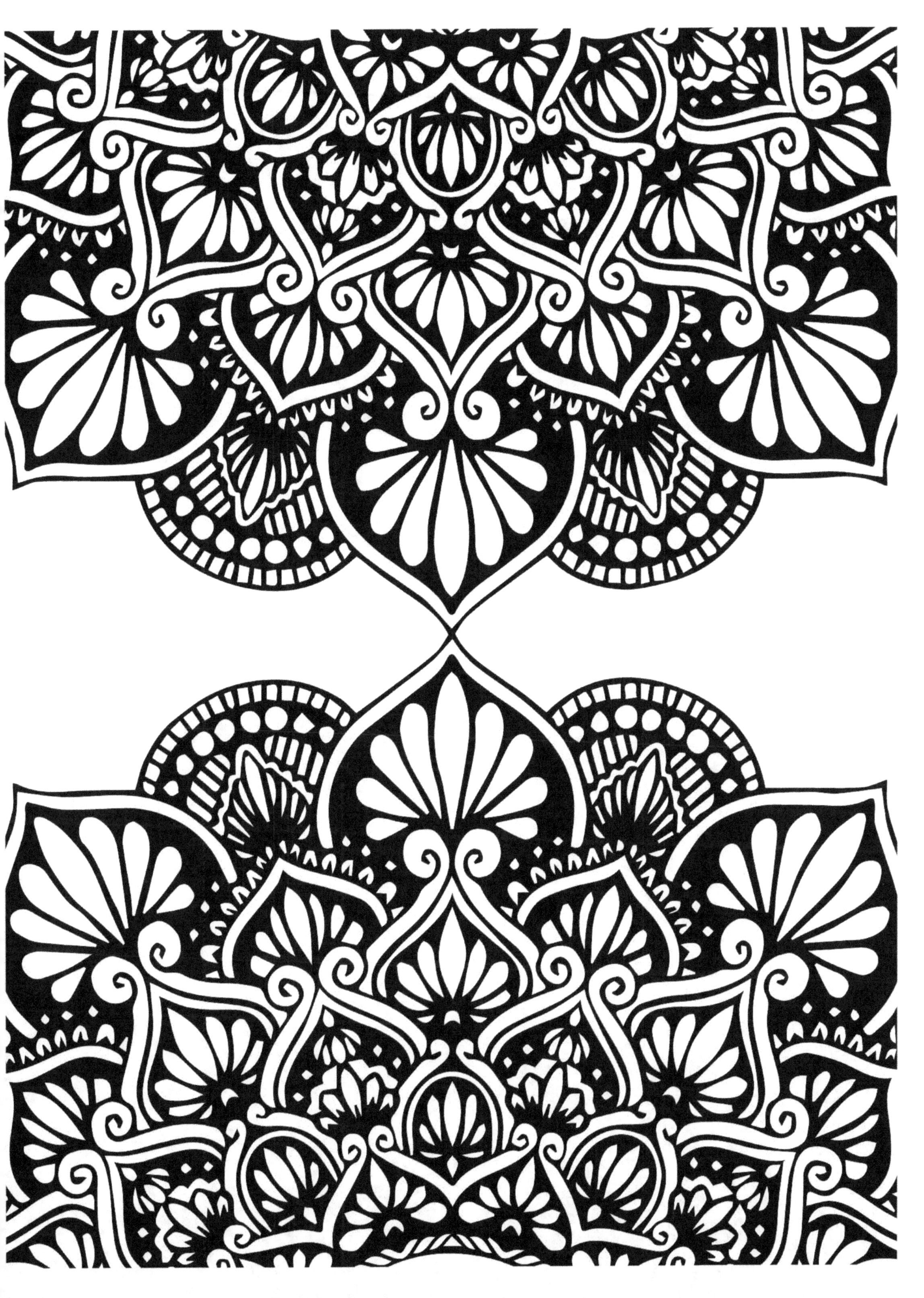

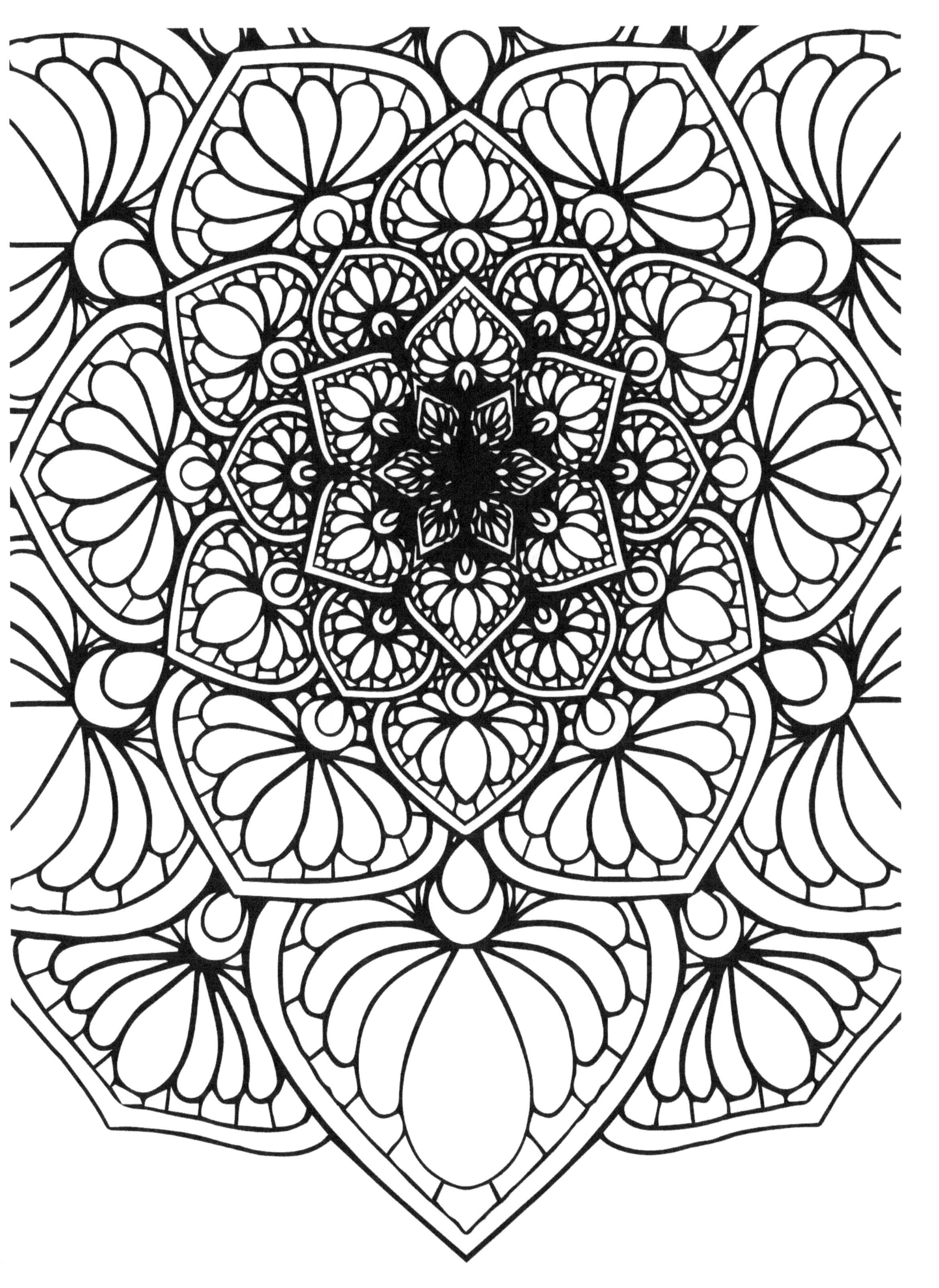

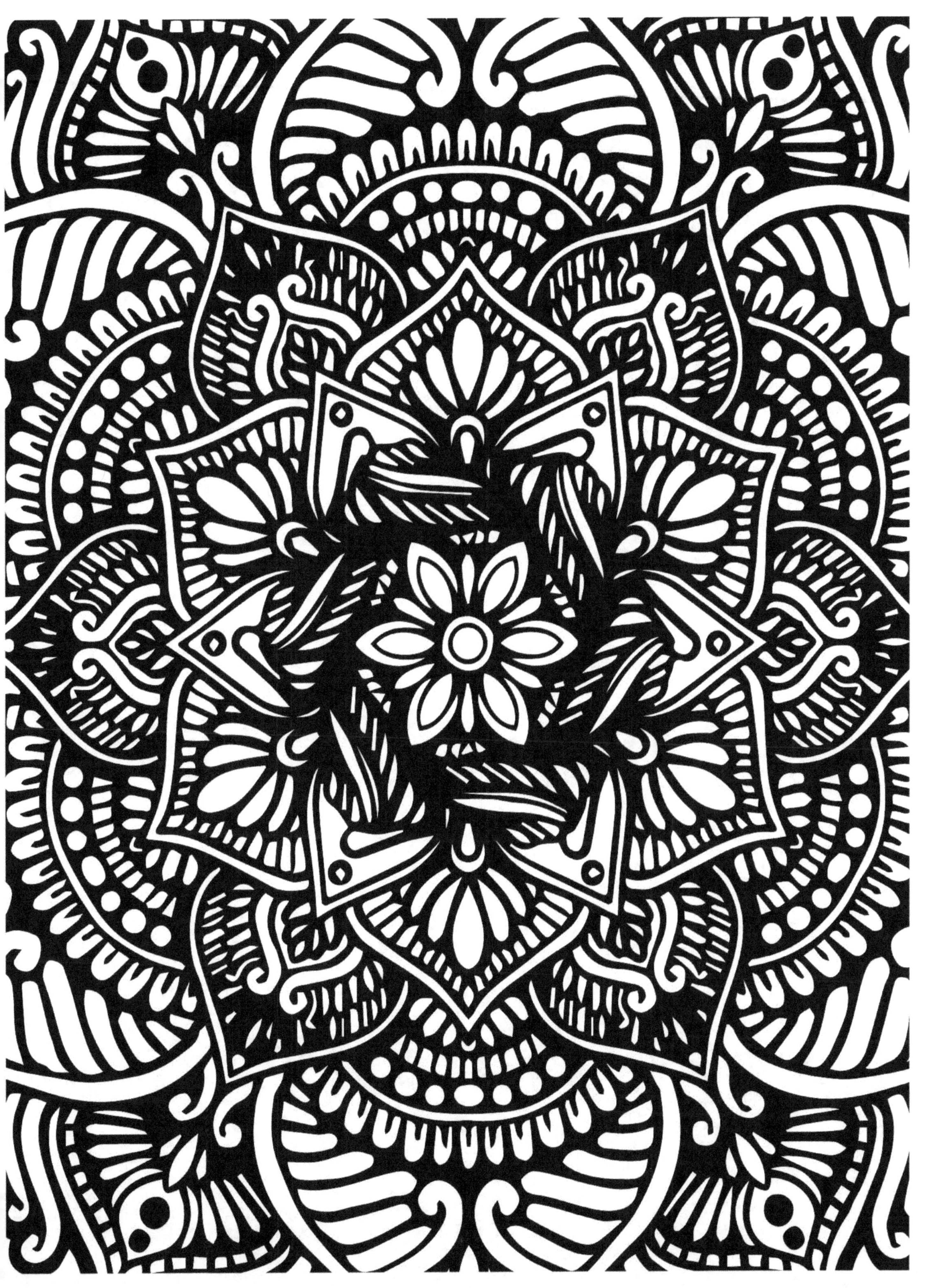

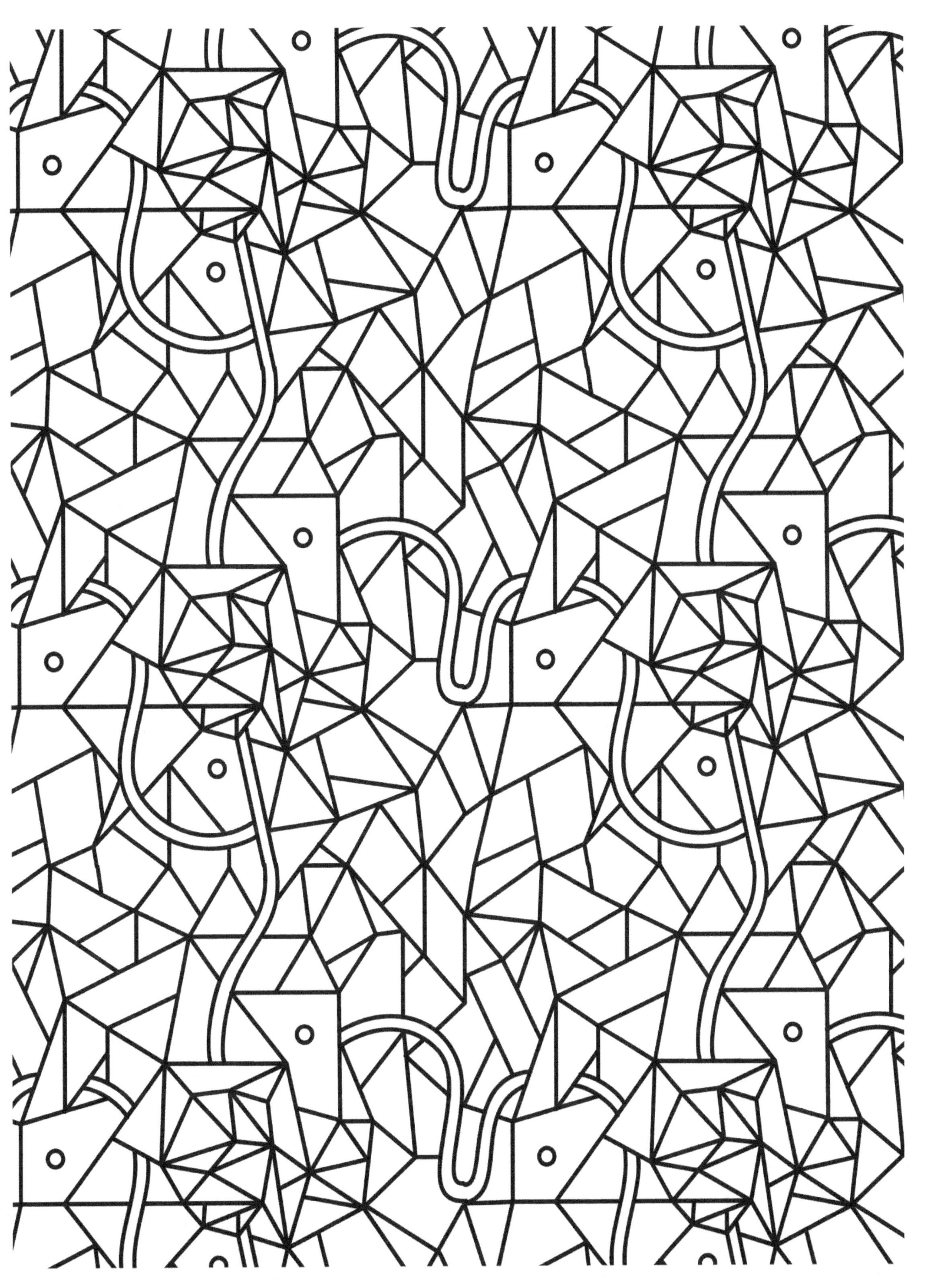

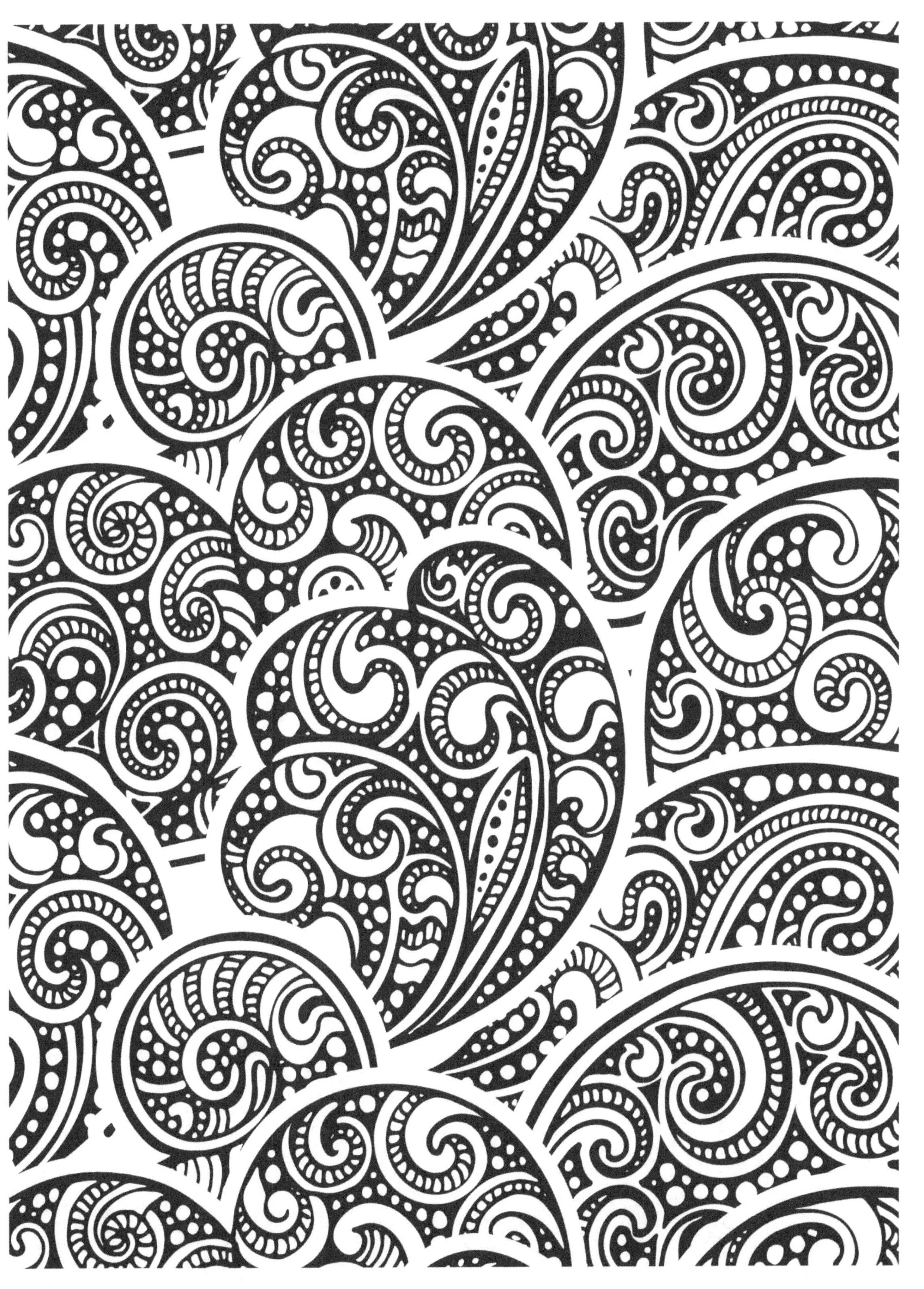

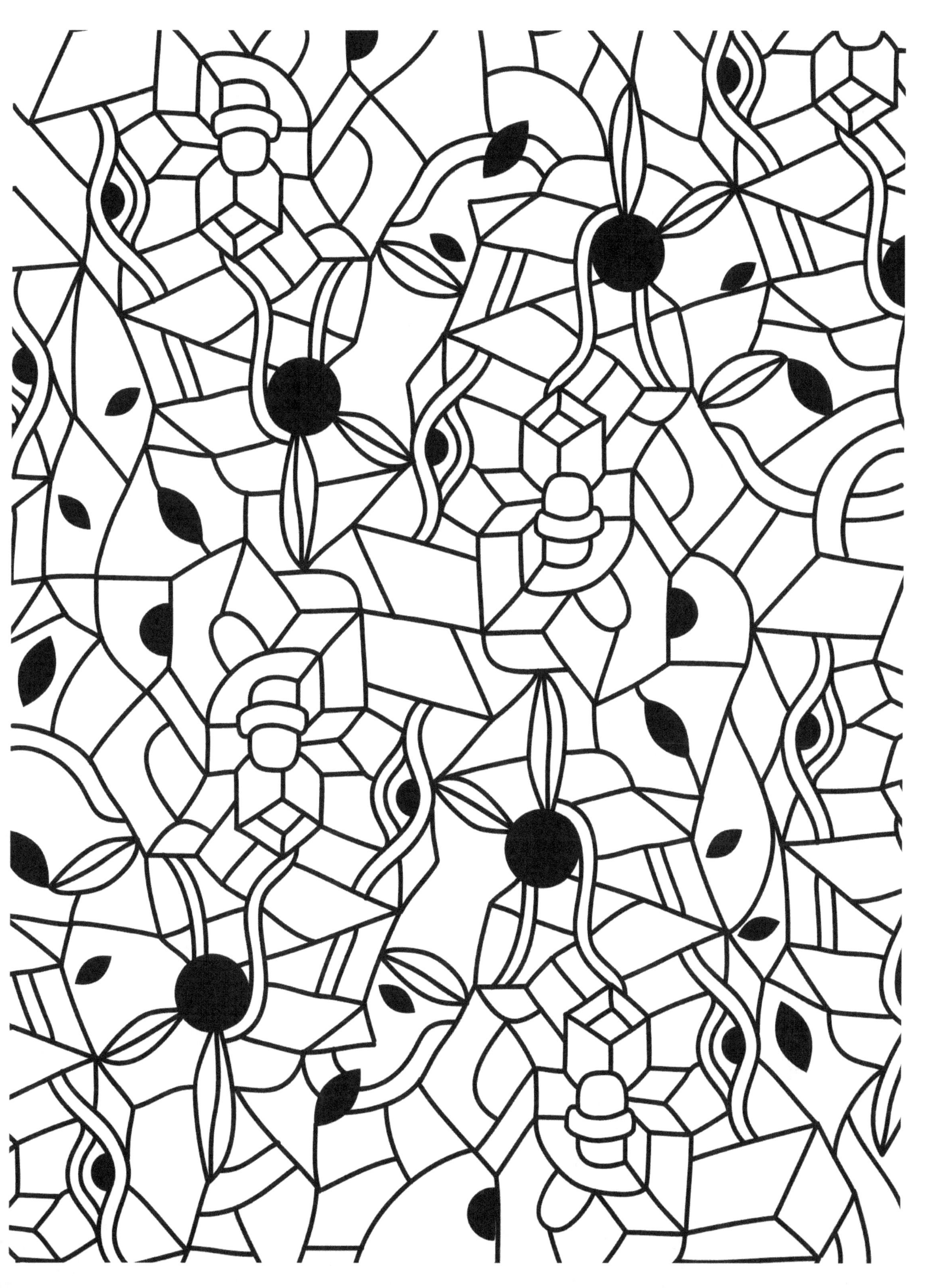

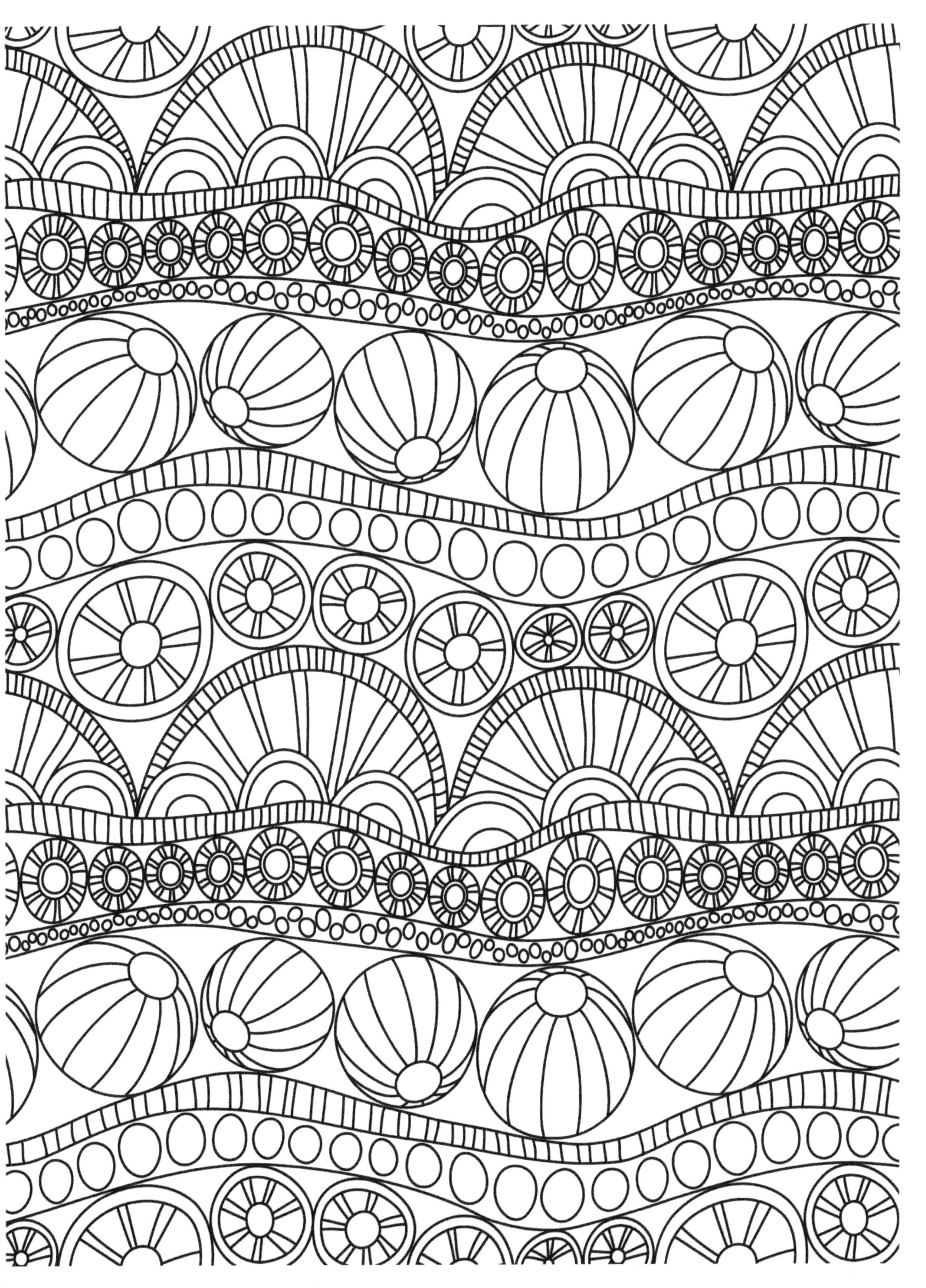

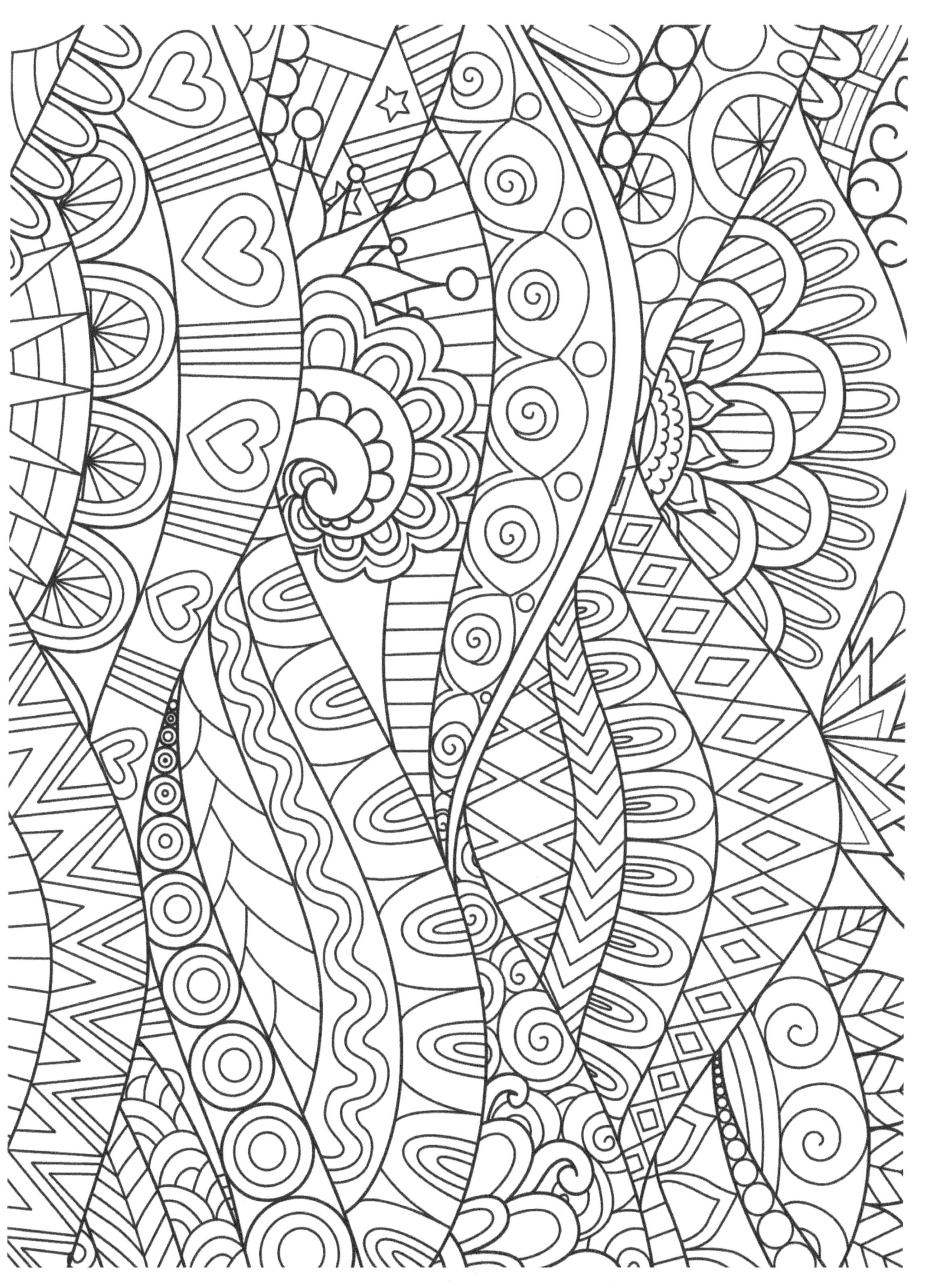

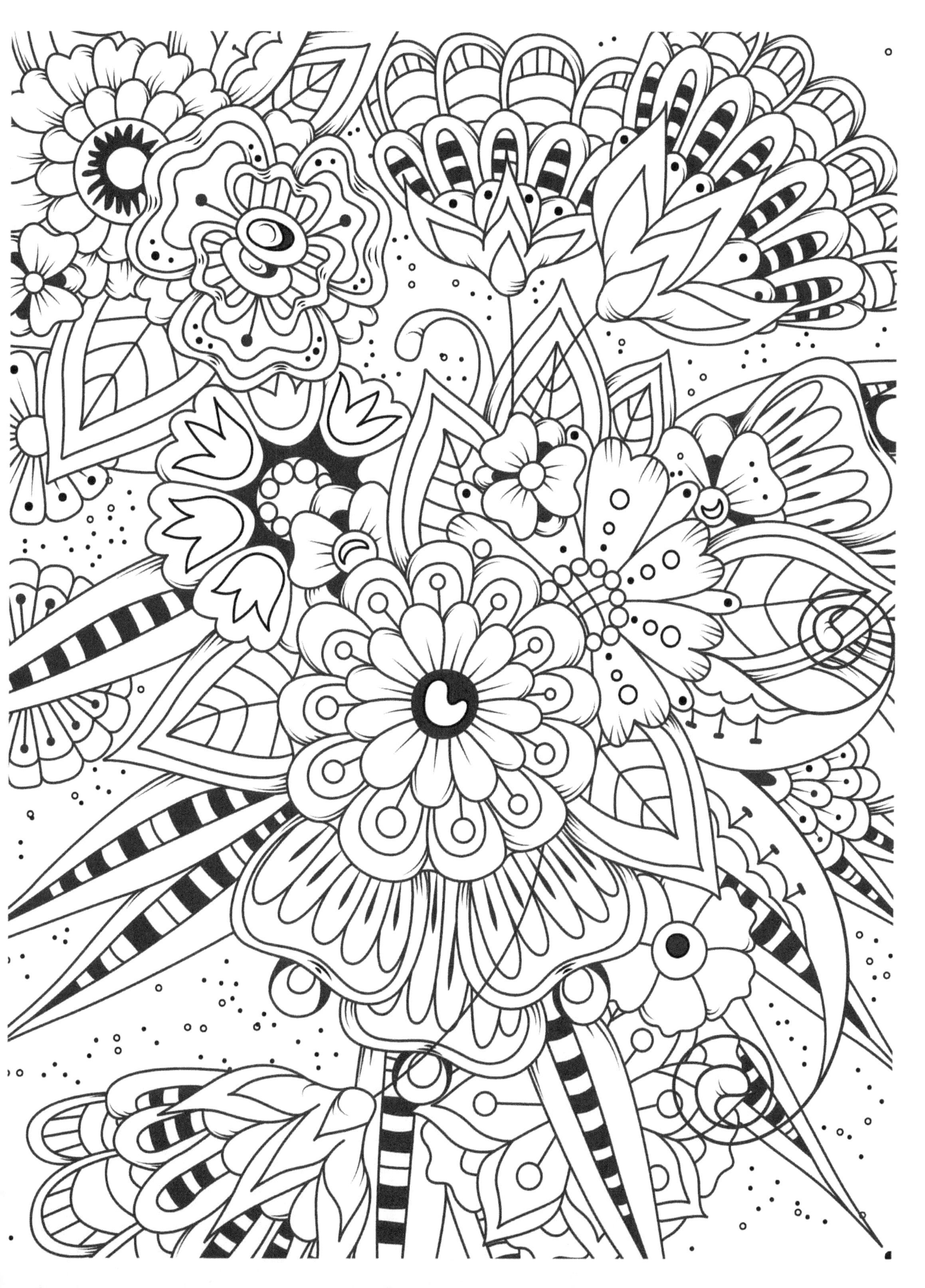

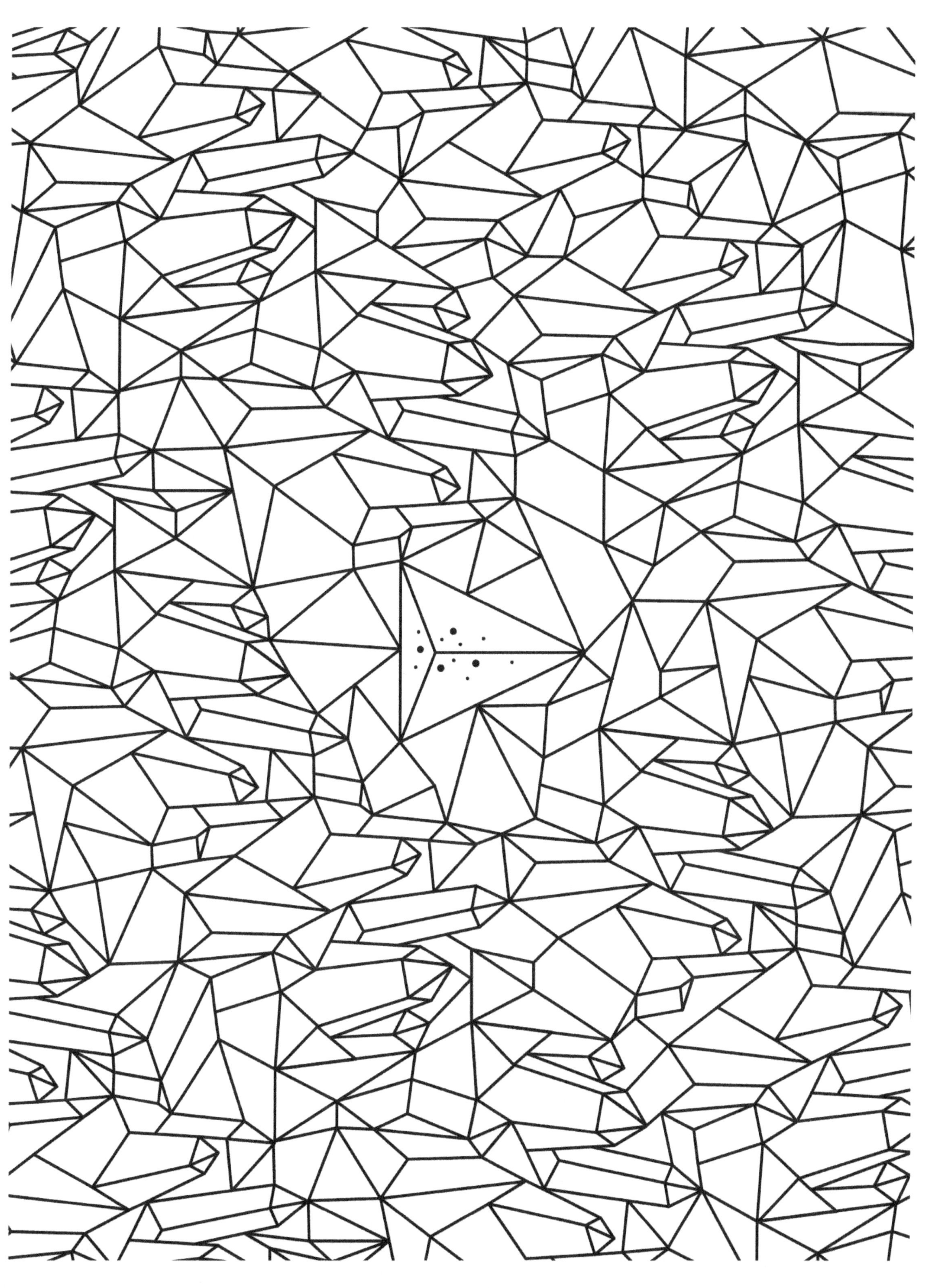

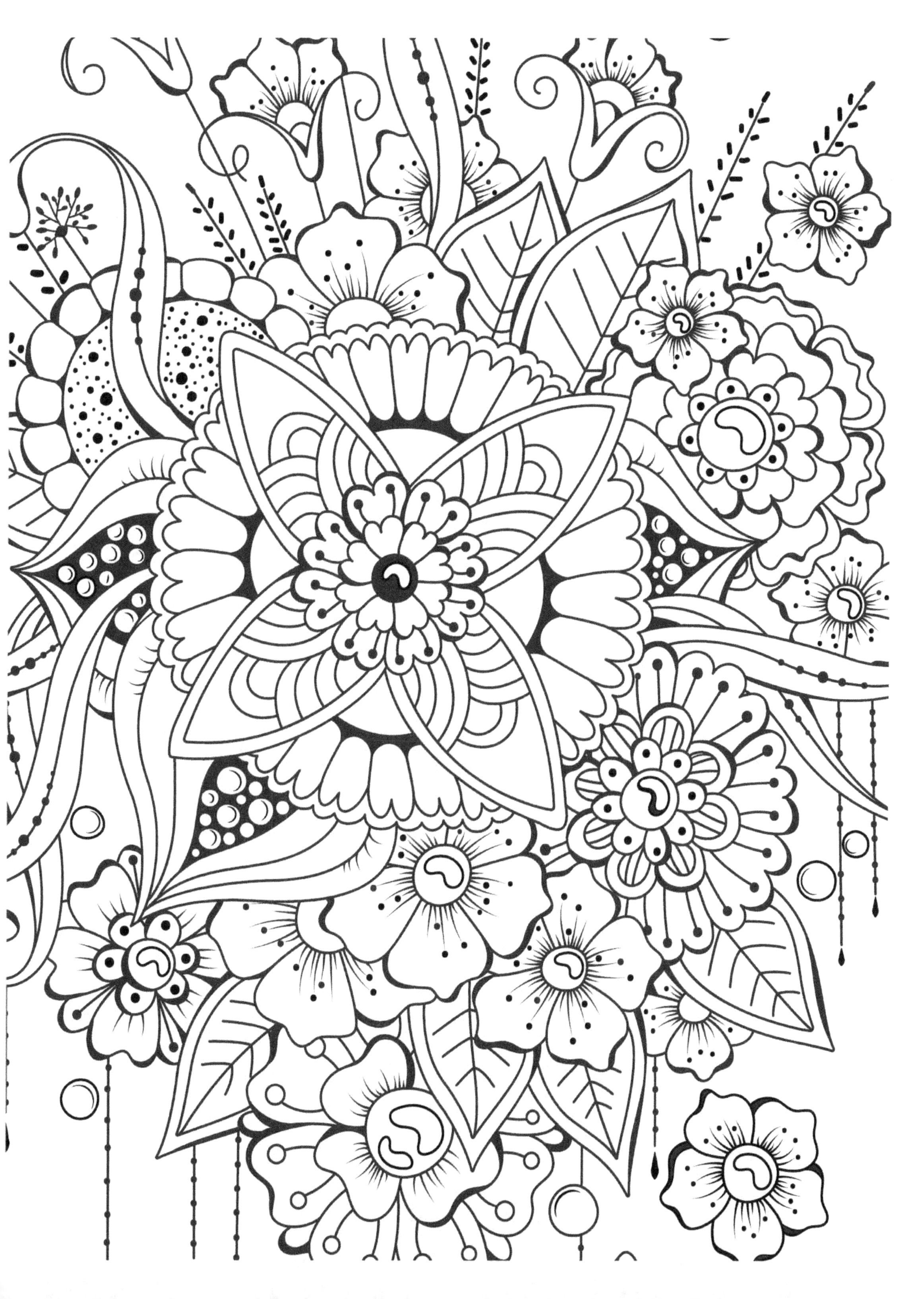

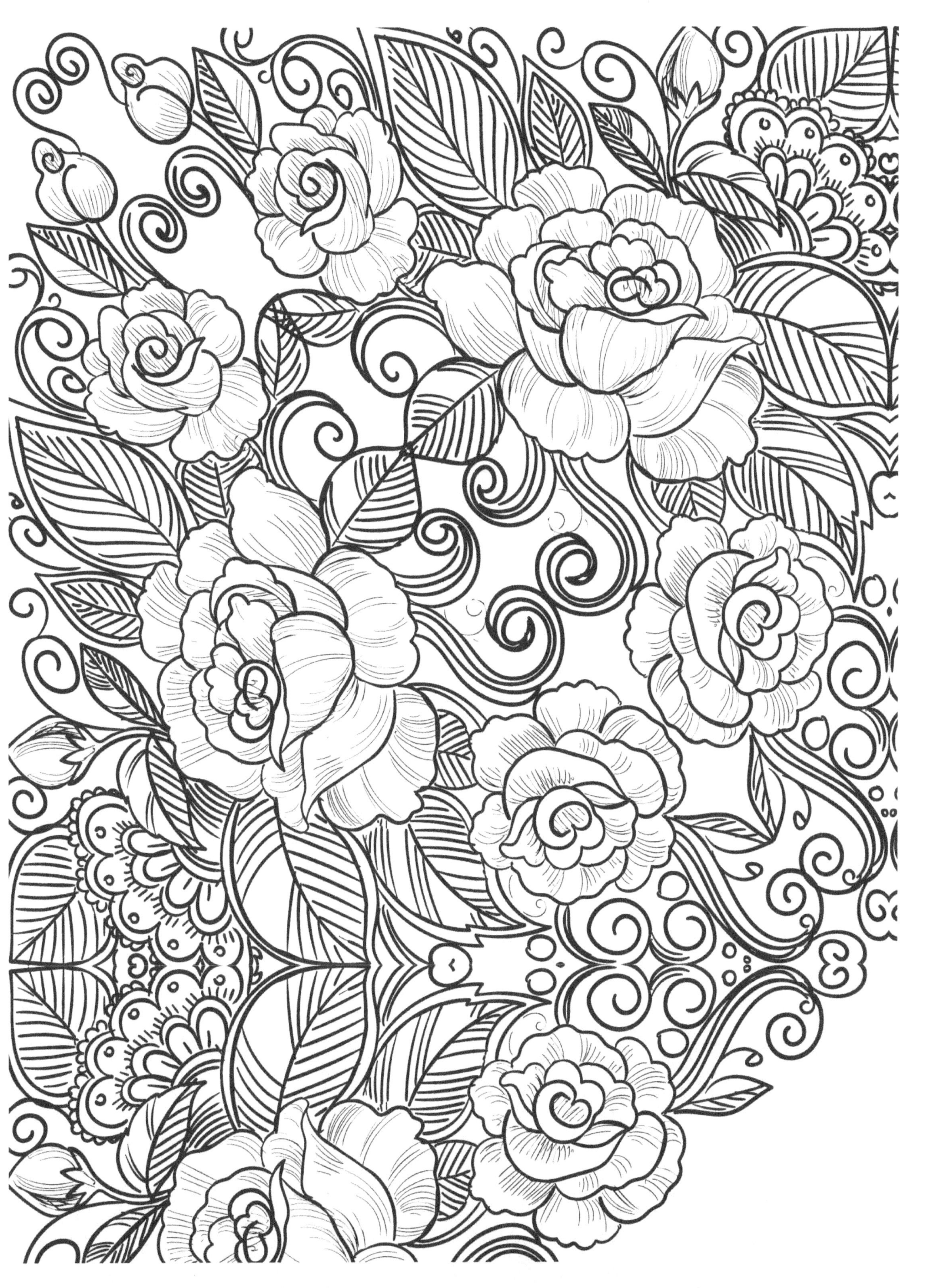

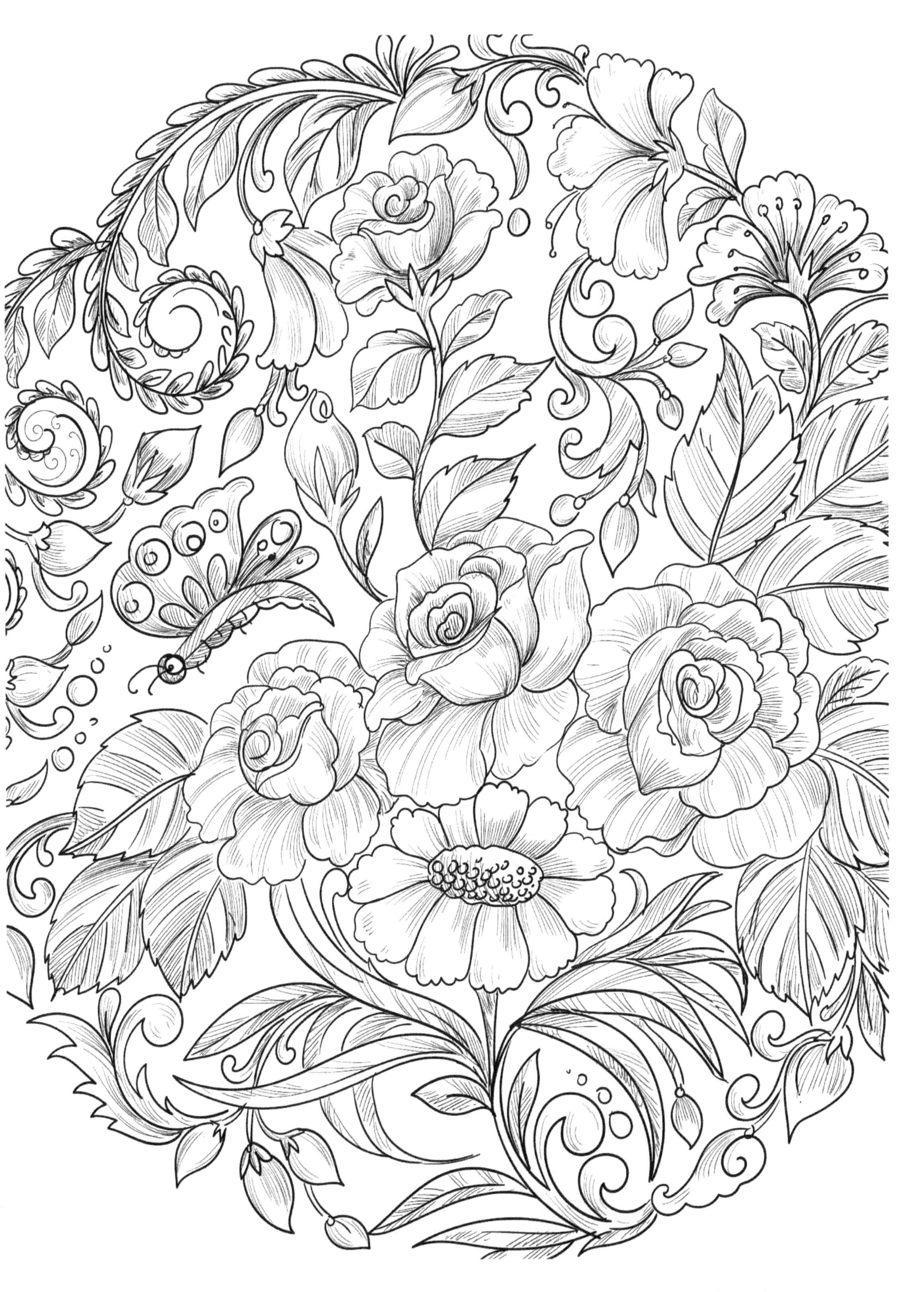

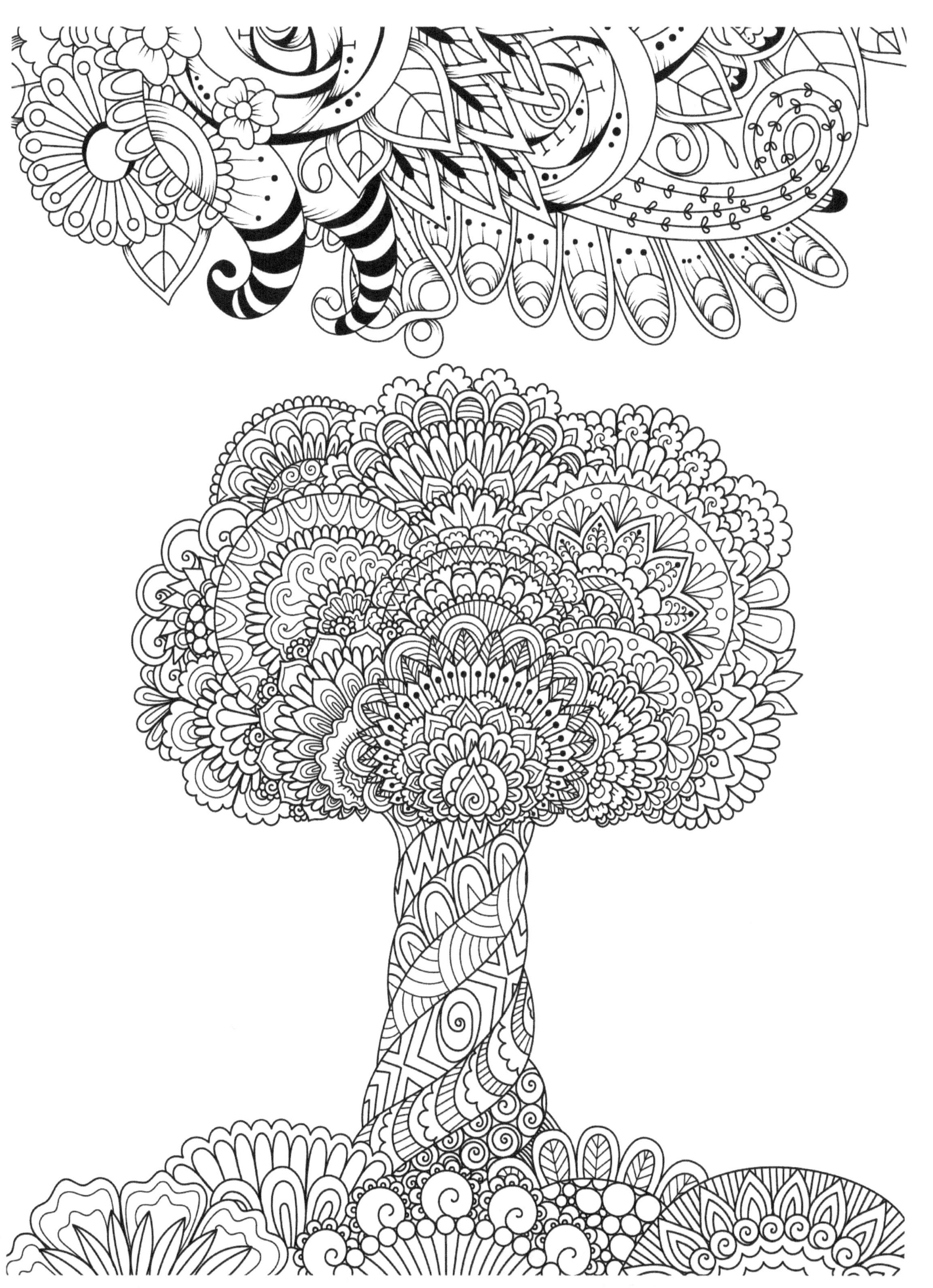

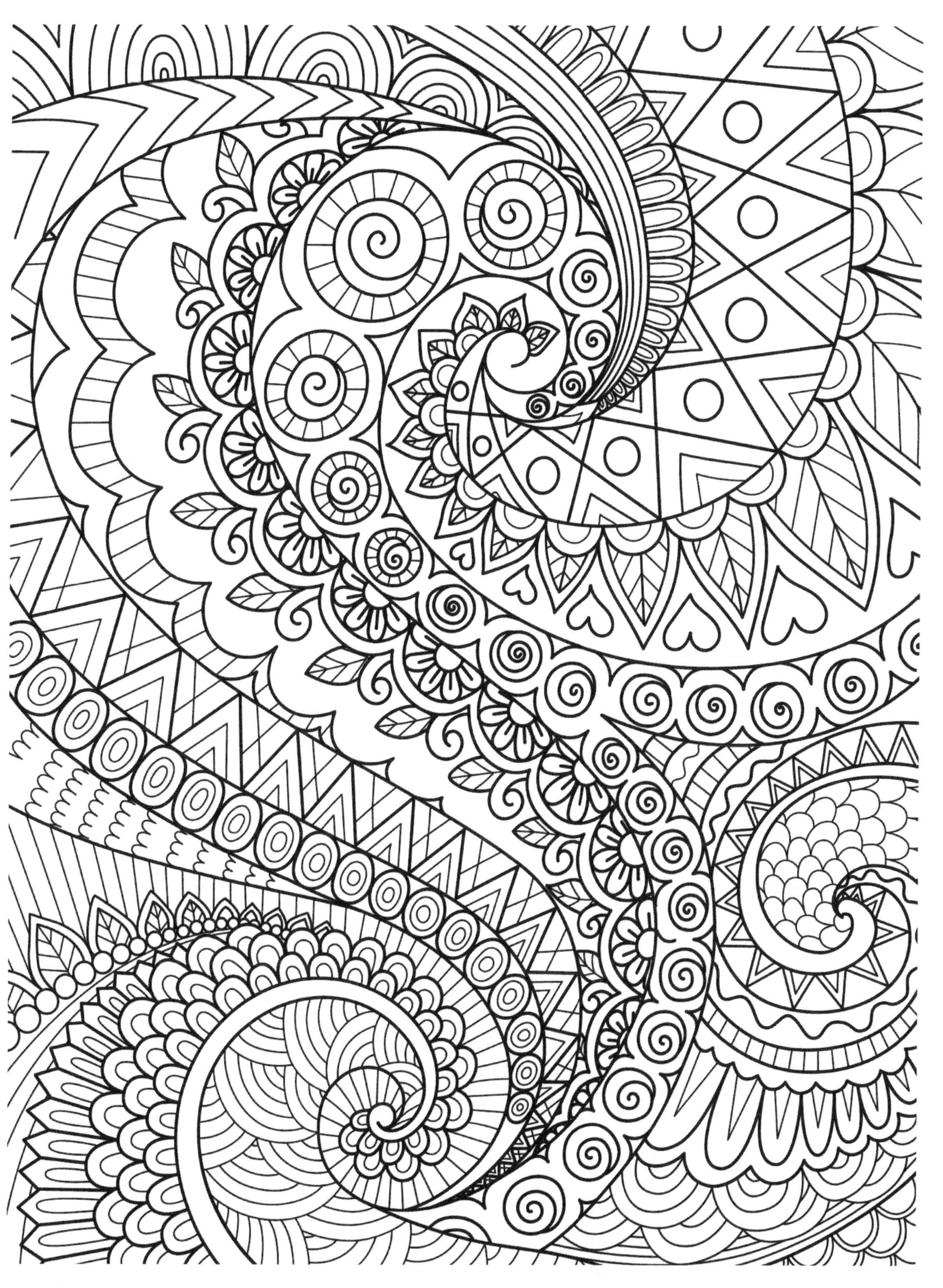

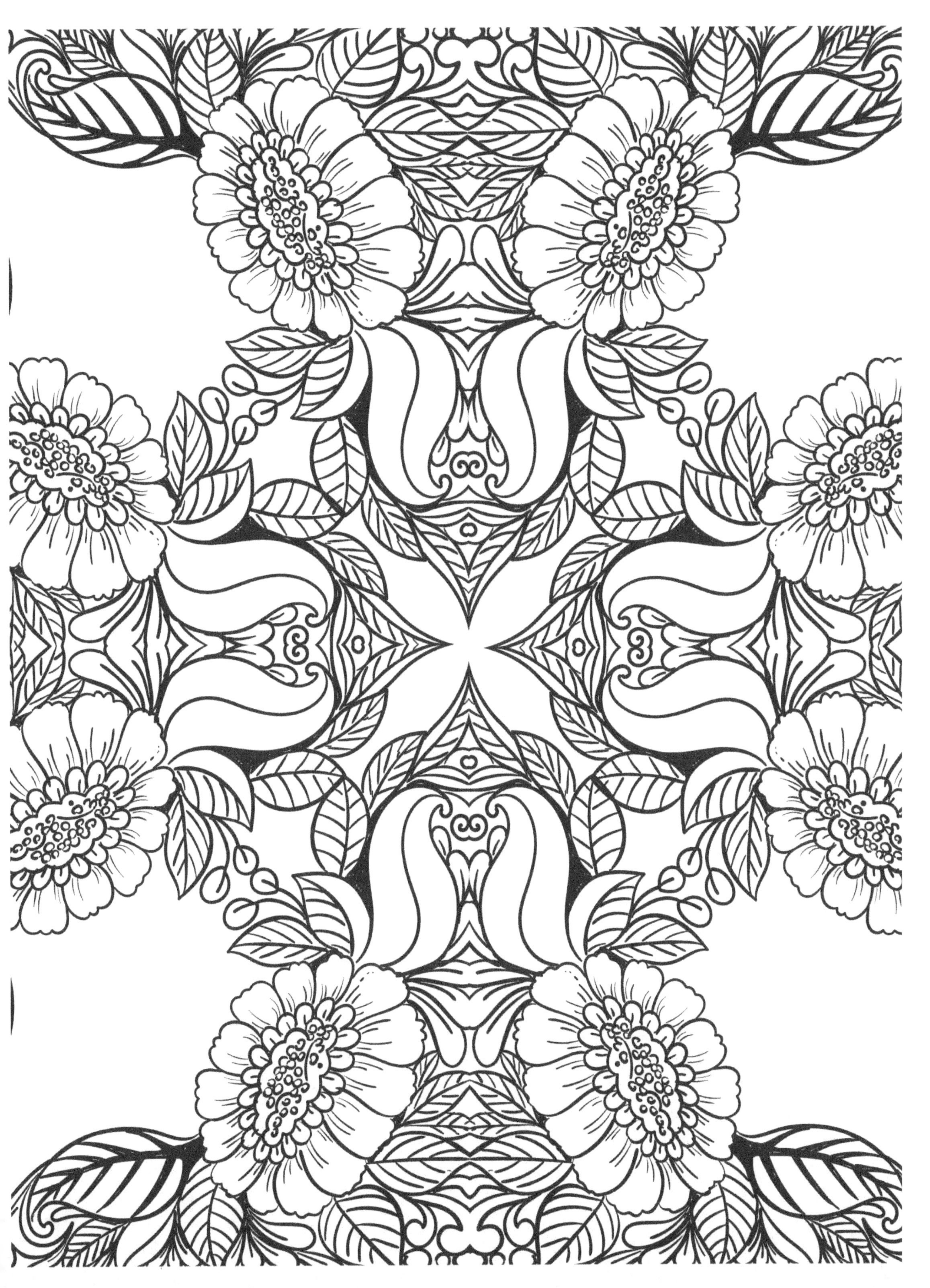

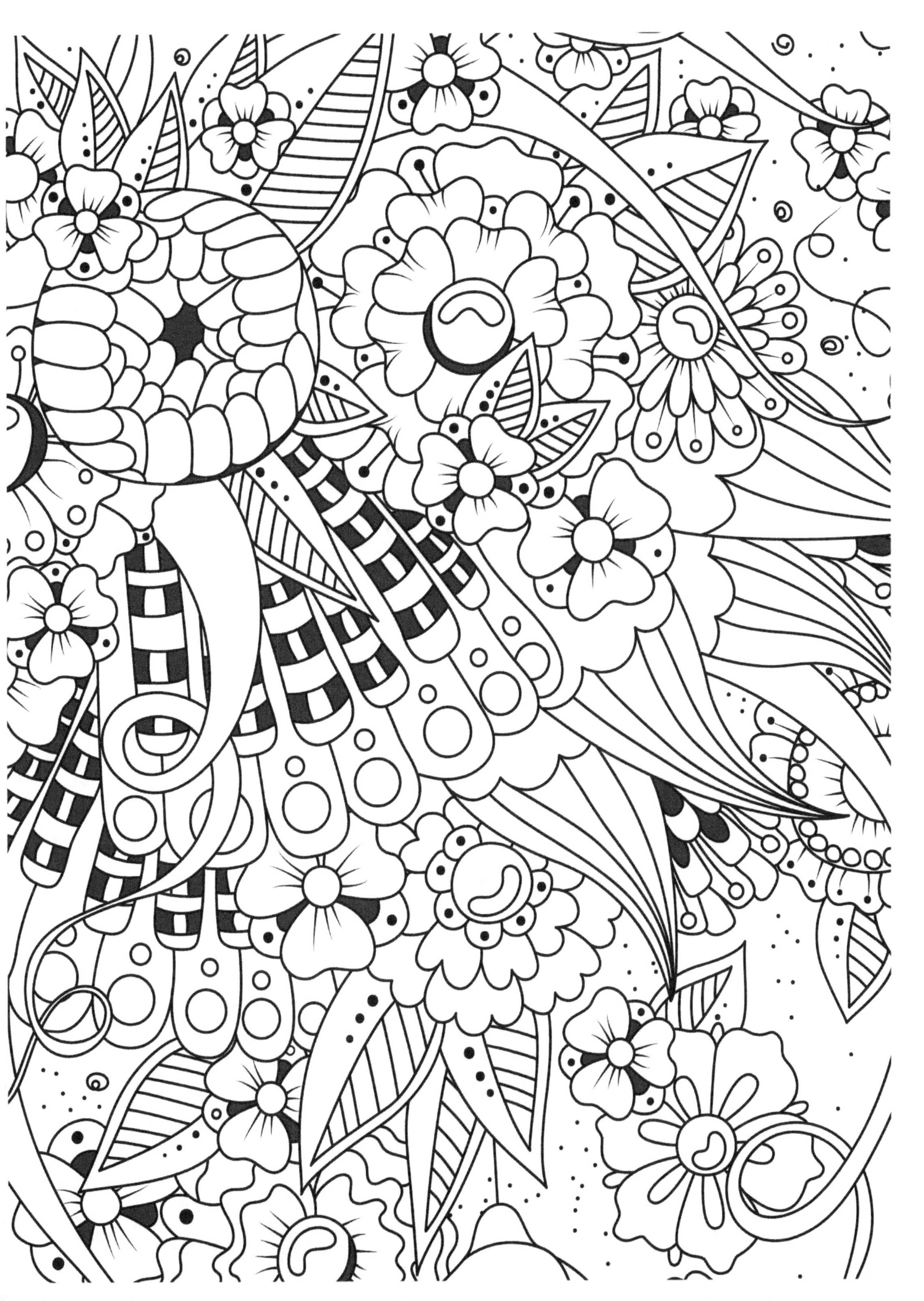

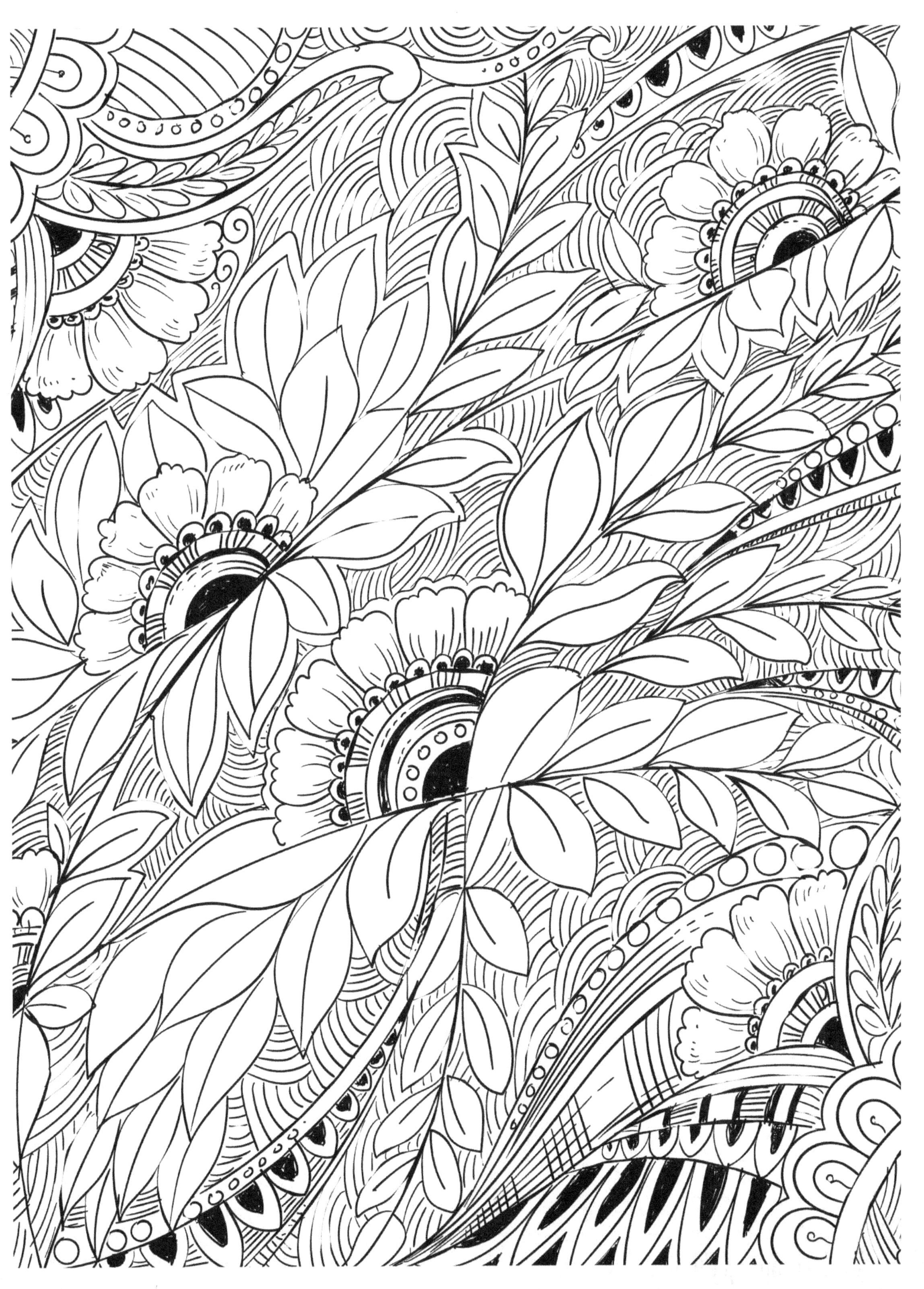

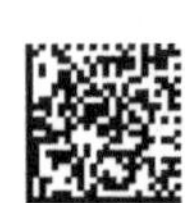

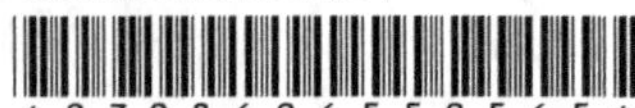